THE LAND AND PEOPLE OF SPAIN

The Land and People of Spain

BY DOROTHY LODER

Illustrated from Photographs

PORTRAITS
OF THE NATIONS
SERIES

J. B. LIPPINCOTT COMPANY

PHILADELPHIA AND NEW YORK

All photographs, with the exception of one otherwise credited, are repro-duced with permission of the Spanish State Tourist Office, New York.

To the two Annes and Arthur

The Portraits of the Nations Series

THE LAND AND PEOPLE OF BELGIUM
BY DOROTHY LODER

THE LAND AND PEOPLE OF AUSTRIA
BY RAYMOND A. WOHLRABE AND WERNER KRUSCH

THE LAND AND PEOPLE OF THE PHILIPPINES
BY JOSEPHINE BUDD VAUGHAN

THE LAND AND PEOPLE OF SPAIN
BY DOROTHY LODER

THE LAND AND PEOPLE OF SOUTH AFRICA
BY ALAN PATON

THE LAND AND PEOPLE OF AUSTRALIA
BY GODFREY BLUNDEN

THE LAND AND PEOPLE OF IRELAND
BY ELINOR O'BRIEN

THE LAND AND PEOPLE OF GREECE
BY THEODORE GIANAKOULIS

THE LAND AND PEOPLE OF JAPAN
BY JOSEPHINE BUDD VAUGHAN

THE LAND OF THE ITALIAN PEOPLE
BY FRANCES WINWAR

THE LAND AND PEOPLE OF MEXICO
BY ELSA LARRALDE

THE LAND AND PEOPLE OF ISRAEL
BY GAIL HOFFMAN

THE LAND AND PEOPLE OF SWEDEN
BY FREDERIC C. NANO

THE LAND AND PEOPLE OF CANADA
BY FRANCES AILEEN ROSS

THE LAND OF THE ENGLISH PEOPLE
BY ALICIA STREET

THE LAND AND PEOPLE OF BRAZIL
BY ROSE BROWN

THE LAND OF THE POLISH PEOPLE
BY ERIC P. KELLY

THE LAND AND THE PEOPLE OF INDIA
BY MANORAMA MODAK

THE LAND OF THE CHINESE PEOPLE
BY CORNELIA SPENCER

THE LAND OF THE RUSSIAN PEOPLE
BY ALEXANDER NAZAROFF

THE LAND OF WILLIAM OF ORANGE
BY ADRIAAN J. BARNOUW

THE LAND OF WILLIAM TELL
BY LILLIAN J. BRAGDON

THE LAND OF JOAN OF ARC
BY LILLIAN J. BRAGDON

---

and others in preparation

CONTENTS

Map of Spain, following page 7

1. A WORLD APART

IF you look at Spain on the map, you understand a part of what Napoleon meant when he said that Europe ends at the Pyrenees. The Iberian Peninsula, four fifths of which is Spain and only one fifth Portugal, does not fit neatly into the European continent, but pulls away southwest from the Pyrenees, that rise like fortifications against France, and rides the waters high as a great ark.

Spain is a world apart; it is a split-personality world of contrasts without and within itself, a gay-gloomy, cruel-generous, barren-luxurious, freezing-burning land. If you travel overland from France to Irún on the French-Spanish border or to Barcelona, the great junction point of the northeast, if you snatch your first glimpses as you disembark from a transatlantic liner at La Coruña on the Atlantic in the northwest or Cádiz in the south, you sense immediately Spain's richly blended and highly unusual nature.

Irún is in the Basque Provinces, home of the mystery people of Europe. The train windows show you moving pictures of this beautiful, well-watered country of deep gorges, swift streams falling down the slopes, old stone and timber houses; you cross roads shaded by sycamores and poplars and see men in blue berets working steep fields. Every neat village you pass has a court for pelota, that thrilling Basque game which seems to send the players climbing the very walls for the ball.

If you disembark in La Coruña, you are in Galicia, Spain's most northwestern province. This is a land of mountains, mist and rain and suggests Ireland or Scotland. Wheat grows in fields high up the mountain sides, corn and apples ripen in the valleys, English hawthorn blooms on the hills among walnut, chestnut, oak and beech trees, and

1

moors stretch purplish-pink with heather.

Barcelona in Catalonia, Spain's chief seaport and greatest commercial center, with broad avenues, superb views, enormous advertising signs, luxury hotels and many factories resembles any progressive European city. The Catalans think Napoleon was not accurate in saying Europe ends at the Pyrenees; he should have said that Europe ends just south of Catalonia. They remind you of their close relationship to the people of Provence in southern France and of the similarity between their Catalan language and Provençal. The very name of their province was given by the French in the Middle Ages: Catalonia, a castled land.

In the Middle Ages, every hilltop there bore a castle. Now, many ancient strongholds stand in picturesque ruins, sometimes forming part of a farmhouse, often abandoned. Goats graze in old courtyards out of which knights used to ride, and fig trees grow in roofless chapels. Catalan towns, those cheerful groups of whitewashed houses with vivid green or blue windows and doors, often occupy the site of some Greek, Roman or Visigothic settlement. Excavations in Catalonia, and all along the Mediterranean coast of Spain still are uncovering traces of the past, such as Iberian vases, Phoenician tombs, Greek, Roman, Visigothic coins, Greek pottery and Roman mosaics. Fields of cactus and aloes, vineyards, olive groves and forests of cork oaks cover the hillsides. The people are handsome, energetic and continually dissatisfied with the government in power.

The Strait of Gibraltar in the south, called the Pillars of Hercules by the Greeks, brings Spain within eight miles of North Africa; you see the Berber Hills against the horizon if you look south from the Spanish shore. Disembarking in La Línea, Cádiz or Valencia, you are in another Spain, a tropical Spain of landscapes startlingly bright under the hot African sky among people marked with dark, African grace. Valencia recalls the Moors and their skill with irrigation. The city, in the province of the same name, lies in one of the garden spots of earth surrounded by land irrigated for a thousand years. When you drive out among orchards and orange groves, truck farms and rice

fields, you pass irrigation ditches and water mills the Moors themselves
may have used; you notice Arab buildings everywhere, see Arab faces,
hear Arabian words and music.

Valencia and its neighboring province to the south, Murcia, receive
about one fourth as much rainfall as Galicia. The Murcians tell you
it rains once every seven years and then enough to cause floods. They,
too, irrigate the land to splendid fruitfulness. The rich, subtropical
vegetation includes cotton, bananas, oranges, figs, sugar cane, olives,
almonds, grapes. In Elche, a Murcian town as ancient as the Iberians,
groves of stately palms produce the only dates grown in quantity in
Europe. The women in secluded Murcian hill villages who still gather
round the town well to fill their water jugs, veil their faces just as their
Moorish ancestresses did five hundred years ago.

Mountains look down on the sea along Spain's eastern coast; some
rise sheer from the water; some are barren; others tapestry their
slopes with pines, cork oaks, junipers and the carob, a Mediterranean
evergreen tree bright with clusters of red flowers. White, amber-wine
and rose-colored cities, many with tiled roofs and church domes glittering bright blue or rose under the brilliant sky, rise above the curv-
ing bays or lie at the water line. Many are centuries old—Gerona,
Tarragona, Málaga, Cádiz among others—cities founded, destroyed
and rebuilt by races which, over the last twenty-five hundred years,
have invaded Spain, possessed it and in turn been dispossessed. This
cycle of destruction and reconstruction is going on in the present, for
cities here as in other parts of Spain were bombed and burned by one
side or another during the Spanish Civil War of 1936-1939, and are
still being rebuilt.

The province of Andalusia is subtropical like Valencia and Murcia.
Burned by fierce sun, gay with low, white Moorish houses, it lies south
of the great tumbled mass of the Sierra Morena (Dark Mountains),
to the north, through which very few passes open. Andalusia was the
province the Moors held longest, and their favorite land. It has Christian churches which became mosques during the Moorish occupation
and then were reconsecrated as Christian churches when the Recon-

quest drove out the Moors. It is a country of olive groves and vineyards, of great estates where the few landowners are very rich and
the many, many peasants working the land are pitifully poor. Below
the city of Seville, fine fighting bulls are raised in the low valley lands
of the Guadalquivir. Guadalquiver is an Arabic word meaning Great
River, and this is Spain's only waterway navigable for more than a
few miles. On the river in the sixteenth century, galleons moved up
from the sea with cargoes of Aztec and Inca treasure from Mexico
and Peru to be unloaded on the docks of Seville and stored in the squat
yellow *Torre de Oro* (Golden Tower) on the riverbank. Still standing,
the Torre de Oro now houses a collection of ship models.

Sherry is an Andalusian wine fermented from grapes ripened in vineyards about the palm-planted city of Jerez de la Frontera, the word
"sherry" being a corruption of Jerez. Many of the growers and merchants who own the vast, white-walled, red-roofed *bodegas* (ware-
houses) where the sherry ripens in enormous casks, are English. The
English have always prized Spanish sherry. Spaniards are proud of
their heady, delicious wine and know the good vintage years and the
poor ones. No entertainment is more Spanish than late afternoon refreshments of sherry (perhaps sixty or seventy years old) taken with
thin sandwiches of close-grained white bread and butter.

The city of Granada is proud to have the Alhambra, the exquisite
Red Castle which the Moors built in the thirteenth century and grieved
so bitterly to leave in the fifteenth. Its courtyards, airy tiled rooms
and watchtowers are haunted not only by ghosts of the Moors, but
also by memories of our own American author, Washington Irving.
Irving lived for a time in the then-neglected palace and wrote his *Tales
of the Alhambra* from facts and fancies which came to him there.
Granada looks out over the Sierra Nevada, Spain's southernmost
mountain range, whose snow-covered summits recall that *Sierra Nevada* means Snowy Mountain. Here, Mulhacín, the highest peak in
Spain, rises to a height of 11,411 feet.

If Andalusia means to you bulls, sherry, gypsies, dancing, laughter
and distant mountains, if Murcia and Valencia are hauntingly Moorish,

new Spanish impressions await you north of the Sierra Morena on the central highlands. As your train emerges from the tunnels and mountain curves and you stare over the bleak landscape of La Mancha where there are more of Don Quixote's windmills than trees, you may remember that Spain is the second highest country in Europe. Here in the central provinces the mountains help to make not only the land but the people. Flying over the provinces of Leon, Extremadura, Old and New Castile and the wildernesses of Aragon, you see a network of *mesetas* (high tablelands) and sierras, white or gray-green patches isolated from rust-colored patches by great, untidy masses of granite, brown or purple or black. Sometimes these mountains climb to ten-thousand-foot peaks that wall off one region from the next. The inhabitants of the central mesetas live withdrawn into the shell of their immediate region. Theirs is a hard, bare, frugal, sober life, little different from that of their grandfathers and great-grandfathers. In their seclusion, they prize old traditions, old ways of life, suspect progress and resent most modern ideas.

Central Spain, though largely poor and barren, is rich in lordly traditions. Most of the nation's rulers have come from it and Castilian masters have imposed their aims upon the entire country. Everywhere decaying cities remind you of a splendid past and a sparse present; they startle you with their crumbling grandeur as they overlook the countryside from some hilltop a thousand feet or more above the plateau. Some, retaining intact like Ávila, their massive, tower-studded walls loom from the distance like ghost cities. Some, again like Ávila, have a fortress-cathedral. The loopholes in more than one heavy church tower served often during Saracen attacks for priests and soldiers to train clumsy fifteenth century firearms upon the besiegers. In once-great cities like Burgos, Segovia, León, wandering in the shadow of haughty houses and high walls rimming narrow streets, you seem to live with history; you marvel at the seven hundred years of the Reconquest, during which, fortress by fortress and city by city, the Spaniards won back from the Moors every scrap of Spanish soil and made the nation whole again.

2. GHOSTS OF THE PAST

As you travel along Spain's ancient routes through the tawny summer dust or the icy shine of winter and look across the open landscape at a range of gold or purple or black mountains, you catch yourself wondering about those travelers who have gone this way before you in the same heat or the same bitter cold, towards the same distant ranges. And suddenly you feel a great press of ghosts about you.

The oldest ghosts are faceless, formless shadows, for we know almost nothing of the earliest inhabitants of the Peninsula. After fifteen or twenty thousand years, very few traces of them remain. Here and there stand huge dolmens (stones set up to form rooms that probably were burial chambers). A few caves contain prehistoric paintings. The best preserved of these are the Caves of Altamira in northern Spain, the entrance to which was hidden by great boulders for some fifteen thousand years. The fact that they were discovered and opened only during the latter part of the last century explains why the reds, blacks and grays which prehistoric artists made by mixing grease with charcoal, cork and iron ore still have not faded, and the bison, horses, boars and deer they painted across the cave roof and walls can be clearly seen pawing and galloping in a very lifelike way.

After these prehistoric artists, came the Iberians (it is because of them that the peninsula shared by Spain and Portugal is called the Iberian Peninsula). About them we know a little more. They were probably nomads from the deserts of North Africa who crossed to Spain over a land bridge that lay where today the waters of the Strait of Gibraltar separate Africa from Spain. Perhaps as early as 2500

B.C. the Iberians settled along the Mediterranean coast between southern Spain and the Pyrenees in northern Spain. Writings describe and paintings on old vases picture them as small, dark, wiry men with long faces, big noses and somewhat receding chins. Many of the scenes on the vases show them hunting wild animals; others show them fighting each other, afoot, on horseback or from the decks of ships. From this we know they were fierce and independent, great hunters and good soldiers.

About 600 B.C. another race, the Celts, drifted down from France until the Sierra Morena in the southern part of Spain prevented their going farther. They were a pastoral people with little culture who, over the centuries, built no cities and left no records in Spain. From other sources we know they were sturdy and stocky, with sharp noses, fair skin and often fair or red hair. Their Galician descendants today have kept these same racial traits. Aside from racial characteristics, almost all that the Celts left to Spain are a few words which crept humbly into the Spanish language—names for such simple things as watercress, kettle, lard.

Over the centuries the two races, Celts and Iberians, lived together in Spain. Often they warred against each other, raiding back and forth through the mountain passes. Sometimes they lived in peace. Gradually, through intermarriage they became more or less one people, a race we call the Celtiberians. The Celtiberians covered the Peninsula and formed the basic stock from which the Spanish race is descended.

As time passed, other peoples appeared. The first two were the Phoenicians and Greeks from the coast of Asia Minor, seafaring traders who drove their frail ships along the long waterway from their homelands and drew together the many parts of the Mediterranean world with strong threads of commerce. They came to Spain as they went everywhere, not to settle permanently but only to exploit the land and carry away silver, gold, copper and lead from Spanish mines. Even so, each of these peoples left its imprint on Spain.

The Phoenicians made less impression than the Greeks, but their traces can be found. There is a dash of Phoenician blood flowing in

Spanish veins today. A Phoenician sense of rhythm beats in Spanish dancing. They brought with them the art of fine metalwork, which the Iberians learned, and they left behind an occasional massive gold chain set with amber or a snake-head bracelet, to be dug up centuries later near a crumbling wall or a ruined tomb. The Phoenicians founded the cities of Cádiz and Málaga, but after a few generations they departed with their cargoes of Spanish gold and their anchors made of Spanish silver, leaving the shores of Spain forever.

The Greeks left more traces than did the Phoenicians. Spain and the rest of the world owe to the Greeks the early legends and first written accounts of "the fabulous land far out to the West." Greek sailors took their ships through the straits that had developed when the old land bridge between Spain and North Africa disappeared— straits the Greeks named for their mythical hero, Hercules, and which we call the Strait of Gibraltar—and then sailed home with tales that stirred their poets to sing and write of the shores and the wild ocean beyond the straits. They told their listeners, too, about Tartessos, a marvelous walled city near a silver-rooted river, whose prosperous and friendly inhabitants traded their rich minerals for Greek wines, helmets and pottery.

Remains of Greek art have been found in Spain and the Greek influence is also evident in beautifully made vases and small bronze statuettes dug from Iberian shrines, as well as in an occasional statue carved by Iberian sculptors. The loveliest statue so far discovered was unearthed near Elche, the Mediterranean city of the palm groves. It is the bust of a young woman thought to have been an Iberian priestess. The statue reflects the artistic ideas of several groups of Spain's invaders. Experts say her heavy, barbaric headdress is Iberian and her clumsy jewelry Phoenician, but they agree that the execution of the statue shows strong Greek influence. You may visit the Lady of Elche, as the statue is called, in the Prado Museum in Madrid, or, if someone shows you a Spanish one-peseta note you will see her pictured there.

After the Greeks and Phoenicians, came the Carthaginians, and they came to stay. The Carthaginians were from North Africa and of the same racial stock as the Iberians; that may be why their conquest was, in general, so peaceful. They must, however, have gone to war with the Tartessans, perhaps because of that city's friendship with the Greeks, who were enemies of Carthage. At any rate, they destroyed Tartessos so thoroughly that every trace of it vanished. Furthermore, after the Carthaginian conquest, the Greeks were forbidden Spain's southern shores. Then the Carthaginians worked Spanish mines and carried away their riches; you see the remains of these mines even today in the province of Murcia.

Still more precious to Carthage than minerals was Spain's wealth of manpower. Carthaginian dreams of conquest became realities because the fierce Celtiberian tribesmen were ready to sell their services in the profession they liked best—war. The Celtiberians lived for brigandage and guerrilla fighting, and the Carthaginian armies offered them an ideal way to see the world. When in 218-216 B.C., Hannibal, the Carthaginian general, marched through Spain and France and down across the Alps into Italy in his unsuccessful attempt to take Rome, Celtiberian foot soldiers and cavalry from Andalusia were the mainstay of his great army.

Carthaginians and Iberians got along well together, intermarried and made common cause. We might speak of the Cartha-Celtiberians if we wanted to invent a learned-sounding term to describe the population of the Peninsula when Rome invaded it some ten years after Hannibal's ill-fated campaign in Italy. Because of this, Rome's expulsion of Carthaginian forces from Spain in 205 B.C. was a bitter blow to the inhabitants of the Peninsula, who revolted when Rome tried to impose her rule upon them. They continued to revolt, so frequently and fiercely that even the Roman soldiers feared service in Spain; an entire Roman legion once mutinied over news it was being sent there.

This Spanish resistance went on for 150 years, dying out only towards the end of the first century before Christ, as wild tribesmen of the interior came to accept Roman law and submit to Roman authority. At last Spain became a united country and a loyal Roman province—in time the most Romanized country except Italy itself. Rome changed the direction of Spain's history, taking away the African viewpoint she had held before and forming her into a European political unit.

Rome built extensively on the Peninsula and many traces of her long stay there still remain. There are said to have been more than eight hundred Roman cities in Spain, cities of fine streets and handsome houses (with central heat), served by sewer systems and protected by strong outer walls—the great Roman metropolis of Tarraco (Tarragona) on the eastern coast had more than forty miles of massive walls about it. A network of good highways covered the Peninsula. Even today in a number of places Roman bridges spanning streams are in constant use. Exquisite mosaic floors have been found in villas excavated in the ancient Roman city of Italica near Seville; excavations at Mérida in the province of Extremadura near the Portuguese border have uncovered a Roman theater seating five thousand people, as well as the ruins of a great amphitheater. Mérida also has the remains of an aqueduct built in Roman times. Segovia, a city sixty miles northwest of Madrid, possesses an aqueduct which is the greatest monument to Roman construction in all Spain—a massive granite affair of 128 giant arches which after eighteen hundred years is still bringing water into the city from the mountains ten miles away.

Rome gave Spain three tongues—Catalan, Portuguese and Spanish. All three had begun as dialects adapted from spoken Latin, but over the centuries, with polishing and perfecting they developed into individual languages. Catalan, despite its distinguished past and patriotic appeal for the people, has become a precious antique. Portuguese (which is, of course, spoken in Portugal) exists in Spain only as a local dialect among the Galicians in the northwest. Spanish, the language of Castile, is the national speech, harmonious and graceful and enriched by numerous Moorish words.

Spain repaid Rome in many ways for the gift of Roman culture. Rome profited by the wealth of Spanish mines, the military importance of Spain's location in the Mediterranean and the bravery of Spanish fighting men. Even more, Spain gave Rome literary and political glory, for Spanish-born authors wrote some of the best Latin poetry, plays, philosophy and history, while seven men of Spanish extraction became Roman emperors.

Inevitably, Spain's fate depended on Rome's. In the fifth century the German tribesmen who were beginning to ravage the Roman Empire fell on Spain, whose countryside lay undefended since Spanish soldiers were away from home guarding other crumbling Roman possessions in Britain, North Africa and Italy. Great Spanish cities, such as Córdoba, Seville and Tarragona, which had outshone any in Italy except Rome herself, surrendered without a struggle to the invaders.

With the coming of the German barbarians, tribes of tall, fair-haired men moved over Roman-paved Spanish roads and swarmed across the land, and one tribe, the Visigoths, remained there as masters. During their early years in Spain, the Visigoths massacred and plundered, spreading plague and misery, but later, yielding to the grace and culture of the conquered land, they settled down to a weak yet easy rule. Spaniards, already a mixture of Carthaginian, Celtiberian and Roman blood, now intermarried with the Visigoths. In time, invaders and the invaded came to obey the same laws. They worshipped in the same churches, acknowledging the Pope in Rome as their spiritual head. They spoke the Latin tongue which was becoming Spanish with the passing years.

However, the Visigothic kings were incapable of governing their subjects well. They could not even settle their own family feuds. As a result, the people were so poor and discontented, and the ruling family so divided by bitter enmity that Spain lay helpless when the storm of Mohammedan invaders threatened the land. Although the religion of Mohammed was less than one hundred years old, its faithful, the Mohammedans (or Moslems) had swept from Arabia across Palestine, Syria, Egypt and North Africa, converting as they conquered. Now from North Africa they looked across to Spain.

In 711, when the Moslems in North Africa paused before swooping down upon Spain, Roderick was king of the Visigoths. He had seized the throne by deposing the former king, Witiza, and banishing Witiza's sons, who fled to North Africa seeking help against him. He had also made a powerful enemy in Count Julian, governor of the port city of Ceuta in North Africa across the straits from Spain. Joining Witiza's sons in a plot against Roderick, Count Julian turned Ceuta over to the Moslems, who used it as their point of departure for the expedition against Spain.

Sheik Tarik Aben Zyad, the One-Eyed, commanded this first contingent of invaders, which landed on the mighty rock guarding Spain's southern tip and defeated the Visigothic garrison there. Tarik named the rock in his own honor, calling it the "Rock of Tarik" or *Jebal Tarik*—Gibraltar.

Although Roderick led an army of eighty thousand to meet the invaders, most of his soldiers were slaves and on foot, armed only with slingshots, bows and arrows. Tarik's forces numbered twelve thousand, almost all of them well-armed horsemen. During a week of continuous battle, the Visigothic forces kept falling back until they were at last defeated at the Guadalete River in southern Spain, a few miles from where it empties into the Atlantic Ocean. Roderick's fate is uncertain. Old Spanish ballads have him vanishing from the battleground, leaving only a gold and emerald-studded sandal by the riverbank, and reappearing later on to fight the Moslems in another battle. Moslem historians, on the other hand, say he was killed and that Tarik sent his head, preserved in camphor, as a trophy to the holy Moslem city of Mecca in Arabia.

Count Julian and King Witiza's sons had strange allies in their campaign against Roderick, for the Spanish Jews, too, conspired against the Visigoths in the hope of ending their persecution.

There had been Jews in Spain for at least fourteen hundred years. According to their own traditions Jews had settled in Spain (they called it "Sepharda") in prehistoric times. Such claims lack proof, but it is thought some Jews arrived with the Phoenicians six hundred or seven hundred years before Christ, and Jewish communities are known to have flourished in trading cities along the coast. The Ro-

mans had been lenient to the Jews in Spain, allowing them to grow
powerful and rich, to own slaves, houses, vineyards and olive groves.
However, when the Visigoths began to rule, this security and prosperity disappeared. In the seventh century, a Visigothic king ordered
all Jews converted, by force if necessary, and their resistance to the
order brought savage reprisals upon them. It is not surprising, therefore, that in the eighth century they were eager to join forces with the
Moslems against the Visigoths; Tarik and his tribesmen seemed sent
by heaven to deliver them from bondage.

3. THE MOORS

BETWEEN 711 and 718, the Moslems overran the Peninsula,
conquering all the land except a strip of territory in the north, where
a few undefeated Spaniards hid like outlaws in caves and valleys. The
choicest fruits of victory did not fall to Tarik and his followers, for
Musa Ibn Nazir, the military overlord of North Africa (Tarik had
once been his slave), followed them almost immediately to Spain.
There, Musa relegated Tarik and his forces to the warlike frontiers,
the mountains and the barren plateau of the center and north, while
he kept for himself southern Spain, the region the Moors always preferred. Musa described it as "Syria for the beauty of soil and sky,
Yemen for climate, India for flowers and perfumes, Egypt for fruit,
China for precious metals."

Although the word "Moors" is usually applied in a general sense to
all the Moslems in Spain, this term is not entirely accurate. A Moor,
strictly speaking, is a western Moslem, a Berber of North Africa for
example, whereas the Moslem conquerors had in their ranks some of
the eastern Arabs from Yemen, Arabia and Syria, who were called

Saracens. Tarik was a Moor, Musa a Saracen; they were rivals and at times bitter enemies. This division between Moor and Saracen partly explains why the Moslem invaders of Spain were never able to knit the country they had gained by their military successes into one lasting, peaceful state. Not only did deadly enmities separate Moors and Saracens, but also each people cherished blood feuds and bitter rivalries within itself. Strong central government was impossible because both Moors and Saracens were fiercely independent and loyal only to a local leader or tribal chief. Moslem Spain was rarely more than a loose web of states ready to break at the slightest touch.

Fortunately for Spain and the preservation of Spanish customs, the cultivated, poetic Saracens and not the wild Moors were the first to hold the balance of power on the Peninsula, and they held it for several hundred years. Saracen love of beauty, respect for science, and tolerance towards the religion of others transformed Spain into an elegant and cultured country. Gradually, during these early centuries, even the wild Berbers felt the charm of this easy, graceful life and began to vie with the Saracens in building mosques and palaces, collecting books and surrounding themselves with luxurious and beautiful things.

In the long, confused list of Saracen rulers of Spain, one of the few clear figures is that of Abd-el-Rhaman I, whom we in the West call Abderraman.

An intelligent ruler, Abderraman introduced and fostered new industries in the land: silk weaving, the manufacture of paper, the fashioning of delicate gold and silver inlay on steel, known as Damascene work and still produced in Spain, the making of fine leather goods which came to be called Cordovan. He took an interest in farming, introducing banana trees, sugar cane, cotton and date palms to Andalusia. He himself is said to have planted in his garden the first palm ever to grow in Spain. He considered gardening a fine art and his own gardens were masterpieces of flowers, shade and fountains.

Abderraman was a great builder. He saw to the repair of old Roman roads and aqueducts. During his reign new palaces and mosques lifted slender minarets and massive walls to the bright Andalusian sky. In 786, towards the end of his life, he began the famous Mosque of Córdoba, designing it himself and toiling with the workmen on its actual construction for at least an hour every day until the time of his death. The mosque still stands. Although a Christian church has been built inside it, enough of the original building remains to create a startling impression of Oriental beauty. Over eight hundred pillars of marble, onyx, jasper, granite, sandstone (even one of smelly phosphorus) sweep out in long avenues, supporting arches hung with copper, bronze and silver lamps. All these columns were taken from Roman buildings in various parts of Spain and southern France and brought to Córdoba by the Moorish conquerors.

In the patio of the great mosque, where orange trees perfume the warm air, it is easy to imagine the brilliant days of Moorish Spain, when nobles were constructing their palaces with graceful, horseshoe-arched doorways and thick outer walls. Within were tiled rooms separated only by filigree-stonework lattices; flowers bloomed in the courtyards paved with marble mosaics, and the visitor heard the sound of running water. There the nobles listened to music, read poetry and wrote it, discussed Greek philosophy, used what they knew of astronomy to predict the future by the stars, studied alchemy in search of the philosopher's stone which men believed would turn any metal to gold. There they collected the great libraries that were the wonder and envy of Europe—seventy scattered through Andalusia and the neighboring province of Murcia, with five hundred thousand books in the collection of a single great family.

While it is true that these Moorish scholars corrupted chemistry into alchemy and astronomy into astrology, all their scientific studies were not so idle. They left many valuable and practical treatises on such useful subjects as irrigation, plant grafting, horse and cattle breeding. The irrigated truck farms and orchards of southern and eastern Spain still keep their memory green after a thousand years.

When we use such words in English as zenith, nadir, algebra, alchemy, alcohol, cotton, artichoke, apricot, we, too, acknowledge our debt to them.

Today Spaniards do and say many things without realizing they are following old Moorish usage. When a Spaniard greets you on your first visit to his home with the welcome *"Está en su casa"* (My house is yours), or when he replies to your praise of his watch or his car or his new suit with *"Está a su disposición"* (It is yours, take it), do not believe your ears; he is merely repeating polite expressions that have been in use for a thousand years. When he praises a dancer or singer with repeated cries of *"Ole,"* he is really exclaiming, "By Allah, that's good!"

For the first four hundred years, or during about half their stay in Spain, the Moors treated the Spaniards more mercifully than any conquerors before them had ever treated a conquered people. Even though they were scornful of their Spanish subjects, whom they considered crude, uneducated and dirty (they lost no time in putting up public baths for the use of the entire population, even in the smallest towns), they were tolerant. Rarely did they urge Christians or Jews to become Moslems. One reason for this liberal attitude does them little credit, however, for they were thinking of the high taxes they collected from Christian and Jew, taxes from which a Moslem was exempt. These cynical rulers preferred larger incomes and fewer converts.

During the first four centuries of Moorish rule in Spain, the Jews enjoyed the good life they had known earlier in Spain. They shared scientific and intellectual interests with the Moors. Jewish historians, doctors, philosophers, bankers were famous and honored in Moorish cities; Jewish statesmen rose to high office in more than one Moorish state.

Christians lived by their own laws, were tried by their own judges and ministered to by their own priests; they worshipped in their own churches or, where they had none, set up altars in the western half of some nearby mosque—the Moslems always kept the eastern half of the building for their own services. The Christian subjects of a Moorish ruler were called Mozarabs. With the passing of years, Mozarabic customs, interest and outlook on life became Oriental, because very few Christian influences penetrated the Moslem atmosphere in which they lived. Some of the Mozarabs were converted to Moslemism, but the great majority clung to their Catholic faith through the centuries. As Arabic came to be the only language spoken in the land, the Mozarabs forgot their Romance speech inherited from the Romans and it became necessary to translate the Gospels into Arabic for them.

When Alfonso VI, a Christian king of Castile, captured the city of Toledo in 1085 his French wife was shocked to learn that Mozarab priests were saying Mass according to ancient Visigothic rites which had long since been discarded by churches in other parts of Europe. They were also reading the Gospels and preaching to the people in Arabic. The queen insisted they change to the Roman rites used in European churches, but the priests refused to do this. Then she demanded that the books containing the Visigothic and Roman services undergo the test of fire so common in medieval times, promising that the one which best survived the flames should prevail. This test of fire took place. When the blaze had died down the old Visigothic books, written on parchment, were found to be in fair condition, while fire had destroyed the newer paper books containing the Roman service. However, the queen would not let the matter end there and declared that now a contest at arms must decide the question. She chose a knight to defend her cause and the Mozarabs found themselves a champion; the trial by battle was held—and the queen's knight lost. Reluctantly, then, she agreed to a compromise: While no newly built church might adopt the Visigothic ritual, old churches were not to be disturbed in its celebration. However, in time all churches came to use the Roman ritual, and today, the Mozarab Chapel of the Cathedral of Toledo is the only place in Spain where you can attend Mass as it was celebrated for Roderick and his tall, blond nobles twelve hundred years ago.

The princes of Abderraman's family who followed him took the title of Caliph of Córdoba, or religious head of the Moslems in Spain, but in spite of the importance their spiritual leadership gave them they could not unite the country—great Moorish cities like Toledo and Zaragoza always refused allegiance to Córdoba. This meant that Christian rulers of the free, unconquered northern fringe of Spain were able to increase their lands by taking advantage of Moslem disunity. They regained a bit of disputed territory here; they won support of a discontented Moorish chieftain in a campaign against his neighboring Moorish lord there. As years went by the map came to look like a patchwork of independent states, some Christian, others Moorish; often one battle or the fall of a single fortress was enough to change the pattern.

Although the Moors maintained no large standing armies, they could for a general campaign bring together a nearly invincible force. Their strength lay in cavalry, for they all but lived on horseback; it was unthinkable for a Moor to be a poor horseman. When war was in the offing, tribesmen from Syria, Egypt, and North Africa joined their kinsmen in Spain. All the warriors were mounted on swift, handsome horses which they rode so that man and animal became a single fighting body. They were lightly but richly armed. Under his turban each man wore a caplike iron helmet; he wore a coat of mail and carried a light, woven-wood shield, a slender reed lance, a sword of the finest steel and a dagger. With the army marched Mozarab and Jewish infantry armed with bows and arrows and slings, but these troops were mere servants for the horsemen and received only half the rations given the cavalry.

For a time in the tenth century a Moorish general by the name of Mansur threatened the very existence of the little Christian states, which had been growing in power. With each season of campaigning he suppressed more rebellious Moorish princes and took away more Christian territory. Driving the Christians back towards the mountains from which they had been winning their slow way south, he penetrated to their most sacred shrine, Santiago de Compostela, in the mountains of Galicia far to the north. There he stripped the church of its precious relics, destroyed its crosses and holy images, and carried off its great bells to hang, upside down, as lamps in the Mosque of Córdoba—an ancient form of indirect lighting.

After his sack of Compostela, Mansur thought the Christian cause was lost and felt sure his next campaign would end all their resistance. Instead, the Christian rulers, rallying their disheartened troops, joined together into an army so fervently religious and so determined that it was able to defeat Mansur and rout his shattered forces. The heartbroken Moor refused treatment for the wounds he had received in the battle and died soon afterwards. The seemingly powerful state he had built fell apart so quickly that within seven years of his death, Sancho Garciá, a Christian prince from Castile, was able to ride to the very gate of Córdoba as the ally of a revolting Moorish ruler. Although the Moor would not permit the Christians to enter the holy city, he sent them home loaded down with rich booty from pillaging they had done along the way.

A few years later, these continuing Moorish feuds brought on the sack of Córdoba by a faction opposed to the rulers of the city. In the turmoil, palaces and mosques were set on fire and many scholars and nobles murdered. Anarchy shredded the Caliph's government into smaller states until the picture of Moorish rule was hopelessly confused. The Christian leaders, being much more closely united and able to forget their differences in a common cause, might have reconquered all Spain by the eleventh century, had they not been stopped by a new invasion of fanatical Moors from North Africa who temporarily strengthened the Moslem hold on the land.

These ferocious newcomers wished to rule supreme. They were fiercely intolerant and began burning churches and synagogues, expelling the Christians and Jews, and murdering those Moslems who deviated from their particular beliefs. And as these invaders in turn gradually softened under the magic influence of Andalusia and forgot their warlike ways, other nomads from the harsh hill country across the straits swept in with new persecutions; these fanatical tribesmen even destroyed many of the great Moslem libraries in Spain.

However, the day of the Moors in Spain was ending. By the middle of the thirteenth century, Portugal had broken away from Moslem rule to form an independent Christian kingdom, and various Christian kings and princes held all of Spain except for the kingdom of Granada in southern Andalusia. There in Granada a long, beautiful Oriental twilight was to linger for two centuries more.

4. THE RECONQUEST

EVEN at the highest tide of victory, the Moslem invaders were unable to sweep over the rugged mountain land along Spain's northern frontier. Christian Spaniards who had fled before the conquerors remained free in the valleys and hills of Galicia, Asturias, the Basque Provinces and Navarre.

One refugee from the Moors was a Visigothic prince by the name of Pelayo, who, having survived the battle of Guadalete in 711, took refuge in Asturias in an enormous cave called Covadonga at the end of a narrow, five-mile-long ravine. There his handful of followers raised him on their shields in Gothic fashion and proclaimed him king. When the Moors heard of this new ruler of the pitiful little kingdom they sent a sheik to Covadonga with a troop of cavalry. The sheik offered Pelayo lands and honors if he would surrender, but instead of accepting the offer Pelayo and his few horsemen charged the intruders as they waited in the meadow before the cave, unable to retreat because of more Moorish soldiers slowly moving into the narrow defile. While the Christian horsemen fought the enemy in the meadow, Christian old men, women and children lay hidden behind rocks above the ravine and rolled huge boulders and tree trunks down upon the thin line of soldiers passing below.

The Moorish force was wiped out, and though the victory seems small in actual numbers of men involved, it inspired the Christians to further efforts. The battle of Covadonga in 718 is considered the beginning of the Reconquest of Spain. Slowly, painfully, resolutely, Christian Spain began to grow again, spreading through Galicia, Asturias, the Basque provinces, Navarre, Aragon and Catalonia in the north, and then seeping south to reach first as far as the Ebro River, then on down to the Duero and then to the Tagus.

It seems incredible that small groups of poorly armed, half barbaric men could succeed in overcoming superior Moorish forces, but one reason for success lay in their certainty that a miraculous champion fought with them for Christendom. This champion was Saint James, known in Spain as Santiago of Compostela, who later became the nation's patron saint and the source of much of Spain's courage. More than one Christian king or general swore to seeing Santiago, before battle or in the thick of the fray, mounted on a white horse, and waving a shining sword. When a Spaniard thought of Santiago his heart beat with patriotic pride as well as religious devotion. The Reconquest was a true crusade, with Santiago leading the Spanish hosts against their foes down the centuries.

Ancient traditions, so dim that no one knows what part of them is history and what pure legend, relate that one of the twelve apostles, Saint James, came to Spain to preach. Later, after his martyrdom in Palestine, devoted followers put his body in a marble coffin that floated miraculously on the sea with an angel for steersman. The coffin washed ashore on the coast of Galicia and there the saint rested until the ninth century, when a certain Bishop Theodomir saw strange lights flitting at night about a seaside place. Upon investigation he found the tomb with a skeleton inside. Visions and revelations, so the legend goes, informed him these were the remains of Spain's own missionary, Santiago.

For fear sea raiders, who sometimes plundered the shore, might make away with the precious relics, they were taken a few miles inland to a place called Compostela, where the people built a rude shrine to house them. As word went about of the miraculous find, crowds of Spaniards flocked to Compostela to pray for help in restoring Christianity to the entire peninsula. Then, as kings and princes battled the Moors, they thanked the saint for victories they won by endowing his shrine with gold and jewels. When Mansur, the Moorish general, looted Compostela of its riches he did not find Santiago's body, for it had been spirited away to safety. Today, a silver box in the splendid cathedral at Compostela is said to contain the saint's remains.

During the Middle Ages, Santiago's shrine became the most important in Europe. Pilgrims journeyed to it from England, France, the Netherlands, Germany, Italy. Cockleshells, his symbol, were to be seen sewed on the robes of German bishops, the mantle of a French king, jerkins of English peasants and cloaks of Flemish merchants. Monasteries sprang up all along the pilgrim route to lodge and feed the travelers, and many medieval adventure tales were composed by monks or wandering minstrels for the entertainment of the tourists. *The Song of Roland* is thought to have grown out of tales that pilgrims first heard recited on the road to Compostela.

Roland owes his fame to Spain, for a Spanish adventure recorded his name in history. The story goes that the Emperor Charlemagne, returning to France from an attack on the Moorish city of Zaragoza, led his army north through the narrow Pyrenees pass of Roncesvalles. Until then, all had gone well with Charlemagne. Zaragoza had bought him off with rich treasure. Charlemagne thought himself out of danger when he reached Roncesvalles, since it was held by Christian Basques with whom he had a treaty of peace. He and his vanguard passed safely through the mountain defile, but the sight of the rearguard, loaded down with rich booty, threading its way through the narrow ravine was too great a temptation for the Basques. They attacked as Pelayo's subjects had attacked the Moors sixty years earlier, rolling rocks and tree trunks down upon the helpless soldiers and shooting at them with stones from their slings and with arrows. Before Charlemagne could send help, half his army had been slaughtered and his treasure stolen. The old manuscript which chronicles this defeat mentions among those who died one "Ruotland [Roland], warden of the marches of Brittainy." That one line in history is all we know of the real Roland, but thousands of pages of fiction have been written about him. Treacherous Moors instead of Basques, the magic horn, the Lady Aude who mourned his death—all these stories grew first along the pilgrim route to Compostela.

Spain had heroes of her own, born on Spanish soil, who fought for her. We meet them in ancient chronicles and in countless *romances* (ballads). More than two hundred romances celebrate the real and imaginary deeds of the Cid, who is Spain's national hero of the Middle Ages, just as Roland is France's. Ruy Diaz of Bivar, an eleventh-century swashbuckler, called by his Moorish title of Cid, or Lord, caught popular fancy and was pictured in ballads as the generous and gallant champion of Christianity and the scourge of the Moor. This hero dared dispute the King, invaded France and defied its Emperor, and went to Italy and insulted the Pope.

In addition to the two hundred romances, there has come down to us the long *Poem of the Cid*, written about fifty years after its hero's death. This work stirs with real life and action. In it the Cid's adventures are reasonable and probable; real places are named and real people and historical battles described.

In *The Poem of the Cid*, when King Alfonso VI of Castile banishes Ruy Diaz from his native city of Burgos, he rides off with a few loyal friends after sad farewells to his wife, Ximena, and their two daughters.

> As when the finger nail from out the flesh is torn away,
> Even so sharp to him and them the parting pang that day.
> Then to his saddle sprang my Cid and forth his vassals led,
> But ever as he rode, to those behind he turned his head.*

The Cid is not idle in exile; instead, he captures one Moorish fortress after another, kills Moors, grows rich on loot, defeats the Christian Count of Barcelona and finally takes the Moorish city of Valencia. Having appeased King Alfonso by rich gifts, he lets him choose noble

* From *Poem of the Cid*, translated by John Ormsby. Stechert, New York, 1938.

husbands for his two daughters, Elvira and Sol. The poem goes on to recount the cowardice and brutality of these sons-in-law, who revenge themselves upon the Cid for fancied wrongs by beating their wives and abandoning them in a wood. Thereupon the Cid goes to Toledo to the King and accuses the sons-in-law of their crimes; the King orders the dispute settled by combat; the Cid's champions defeat the two cowards and Elvira and Sol are later on consoled by more worthy, royal husbands.

Old Spanish and Moorish chroniclers agree with the ballads and the *Poem of the Cid* in calling the Cid a man of courage, but the histories do not idealize him. For all his bravery, they show him as cruel and treacherous, willing to sell his services to any Moslem ruler who pays well and not hesitating to betray the Moorish King who entrusts him with the siege of Valencia. Once he has captured the starving city, he keeps it for himself. But before we judge this medieval hero by our modern standards of wrong and right, we must recall that in his day both Christians and Moslems admired trickery, especially against an enemy. Even the Arab chroniclers who call Ruy Diaz "the scourge of the land" admit he was "a marvel of the Lord in love of glory, strength of character and courage."

The Moors retook Valencia three years after the Cid's death and held it for three centuries more. Christian Spain was no richer in lands or castles because of him, and yet this selfish, ambitious man was the hero and inspiration of many who waged an unselfish fight for Spain. Tales of his deeds encouraged nobles, priests and peasants to fight on, even when Moslem enemies threatened to destroy all the gains they had made.

By the eleventh century, the Kingdom of Castile had slowly collected and put together enough broken bits of territory to make itself the strongest Christian state in Spain. Alfonso VI, the Cid's overlord (you recall his queen's campaign against the Mozarab church services) had captured Toledo in 1085. Alfonso, a man of ideas and imagination, was more tolerant than his predecessors and most of his contemporaries, who believed in enslaving the Moslem inhabitants of all the territory they conquered. Alfonso had observed how satisfied the Mozarabs seemed under tolerant Moorish rule. Therefore, when he took Toledo, he treated the Moors in the city with honor and fairness. Other Christian princes realized that contented subjects were less likely to revolt, and they began to follow Alfonso's example.

Gradually small independent Christian states began combining through wars, treaties and royal marriages into larger states until, like pieces in a jigsaw puzzle, they formed an increasingly united Spain. Early in the thirteenth century, Alfonso VIII of Castile allied himself with the Kings of Navarre and Aragon and led their combined armies south through a secret pass in the Sierra Morena range to fall upon a united Moorish host as it lay encamped on a sloping plain known as the Navas de Tolosa. They destroyed it completely. The battle of the Navas de Tolosa marked the end of Moorish predominance on the Peninsula. Less than twenty years later the King of Aragon (who was equally proud to be also the Count of Barcelona), captured Majorca, Minorca and Ibiza, the delightful Balearic Islands off the Mediterranean coast which are still part of Spain.

The longest single step towards Spanish unity was the marriage in 1469 of Ferdinard, heir to the crown of Aragon, with Isabella, the heiress of Castile. Both of the Catholic Monarchs, as they came to be called, were ambitious: Ferdinand for boundless political power and wider lands to rule, and Isabella for a Spain so Catholic that not one Moorish or Jewish prayer should stir its air. They were determined to consolidate Spain into a great Catholic nation and their thoughts turned to Granada, the last Moorish kingdom remaining on the Peninsula. To be sure, Granada was a weak little state which had long been subject to Castile (its Moorish king had signed as one of the official witnesses to the wedding of Ferdinand and Isabella). Its rulers in their lovely red palace of the Alhambra, with little more than local affairs to attend to, led lives of ease and pleasure. They went hunting and hawking in the mountains and meadows about the city. They entertained scholars from Africa and the Near East, who came to sit with them in a patio beside a pool or in a garden near a fountain and to read poetry and discuss philosophy. Their lives sounded harmless and charming. But town and palace teemed with intrigue and treachery. Sometimes political murders spattered the mosaic floors of the Alhambra with blood. Sometimes, too, a dissatisfied prince of Granada broke faith with Castile to raid Christian lands. Now and then North African adventurers plotting larger expeditions against the Christians were sheltered within the city's walls.

Ferdinand and Isabella saw that this infidel wedge kept them from uniting Spain, and they determined to remove it. The rulers began planning war. Priests and bishops preached the conquest of Granada. The people spoke of the coming expedition as a holy war. At last, in 1491, after years of preparation, Ferdinand led fifty thousand men to besiege the city. The Queen and her children followed the army and settled down in a village of low stone houses built for them just beyond the walls of Granada, which the Queen called *Santa Fé* (Holy Faith). Here they lived for months while Ferdinand and his army harried the Moorish forces venturing from the city, laid waste the land round about and cut off all food supplies from the besieged inhabitants of Granada. The Queen ran the risks of war—she even wore armor, which can be seen today in the Royal Armory in Madrid. Once she narrowly missed being stabbed by a fanatical Moor. Another time, her curiosity about the Alhambra almost led her into Moorish captivity. She had climbed to the roof of a house in a nearby village to catch a glimpse of the fabulous palace when a body of enemy cavalry surrounded the building and were about to enter. Her own horsemen arrived just in time to drive them off.

After months of siege, hungry Granada surrendered. In January, 1492, a silver cross was raised above the Alhambra as Ferdinand and Isabella made their solemn entry into the city. The struggle Pelayo had begun at Covadonga in 718 ended at Granada 774 years later.

5. CONQUISTADORES

THREE months after the conquest of Granada, Ferdinand and Isabella expelled the Jews from Spain, claiming the nation would be more unified and safer without them. They feared that the Jews, if they grew dissatisfied, might conspire with the Moors in North Africa, as they had done in 711, to bring about a new invasion of Spain. Stripped of their wealth, the Jews scattered to countries along the southern shores of the Mediterranean, where even today their descendants boast of a Spanish past.

A third event in Spanish history even more significant for the world than the conquest of Granada or the expulsion of the Jews took place in the same year. On October 12, 1492, Christopher Columbus discovered the New World.

Although Queen Isabella had been interested for a number of years in Columbus' theory that he could find a sea route to the Far East by sailing west, she had been unable to help him because she needed all her revenues for the war against the Moors in Granada. Not until the Spaniards were victorious could she think of Columbus and his venture, but soon afterwards, in April, 1492, while still at Santa Fé, she signed the contract with him authorizing his voyage. She had no ready cash for the enterprise, but she did not sell her jewels as the legend goes; instead, she ordered the little seaport town of Palos to equip and man two sailing vessels as a fine "for certain things done and committed" and turn them over to Columbus. (The inhabitants of the town grumbled loudly at such punishment.) Two brothers from Palos, Martín and Vicente Pinzón, supplied the third ship.

If you go to Palos now (it lies fifty miles southwest of Seville by good road through farm lands and orchards) you find a small, neglected fishing village, little changed since Columbus' time. Though the worse for wear, its ancient church of San Jorge still stands; the priest preaches from the same iron pulpit from which royal authority for the voyage was proclaimed early on the morning of August 3, 1492. This was the last Mass that Columbus, his captains and men were to attend on land for months to come. After Mass, the adventurers marched in a body from the white town down to the shore, where three light sailing ships were moored. Imagine how the inhabitants crowded the waterfront to watch their departure!

We have heard of the hardships and uncertainties of that first transatlantic trip and we can imagine with what joy the voyagers went ashore on a small island in the Bahamas on October twelfth. Columbus took possession of the new land in the name of Isabella, calling it San Salvador. He had no idea he was in the shadow of two vast continents. On the third of the four voyages he made to the New World, he actually landed on the mainland of South America, but did not realize he had discovered a whole new world. He died believing he had reached India by water. That is why Spaniards of the fifteenth, sixteenth and seventeenth centuries spoke of North and South America and the islands of the Caribbean by the general term "Indies."

Legally, the Indies belonged to Isabella and the Crown of Castile, not to Ferdinand, for it was she and not her husband who had believed in and helped Columbus. Ferdinand lent a little money for the first expedition, but on condition he be repaid every bit whether the venture failed or not; if it succeeded he was to receive repayment many times greater than his loan. Consequently Columbus' four voyages to the Western Hemisphere were strictly Castilian ventures. Ferdinand's own subjects in Catalonia and Aragon were not permitted to go along even though Catalans were Spain's most experienced sailors and until then had brought the nation most of its naval glory. This Castilian monopoly continued after Isabella's death, for her will provided that her people, only, should enjoy the right to explore, settle and trade with the Indies. Now and again the ban was lifted in an individual case, but in general it continued to hold for three hundred years.

When Columbus and his men came home in March, 1493, their tales thrilled the Spaniards of their day. With the nation at peace, life had begun to seem flat and dull, and men long used to danger and tension, welcomed the challenge of new adventures. They dreamed of fabulous wealth beyond strange oceans; their zeal for spreading the Catholic faith now burned for the natives of the New World. All ages and types of men flocked to join expeditions being organized to the Indies. Sailors, professional soldiers, shopkeepers, farmers, scholars, nobles, rascals and priests sailed off together to explore, settle, exploit and convert those lands which are now the West Indies, Mexico and the southern borders of the United States, Central America, and much of South America. They met various fates, some dying of fever or poisoned arrows in jungles and swamps, some winning rich land grants and building palaces strong as fortresses in New World settlements, others acquiring fortunes in gold and jewels and returning to live like lords in castles in Spain.

They left brillant records behind them that you can see if you visit the Archives of the Indies in Seville. This magnificent library of documents relating to discoveries, conquest and colonization in the New World was begun by Columbus' son Fernando and left by him to the nation. What courage speaks from these yellowed letters and reports, what hardships follow every mile of the ancient colored maps! No wonder the men who wrote from wilderness outposts and drew up maps as they struggled through impenetrable forests and over mountain passes are known to history as *Conquistadores*. It is the Spanish word meaning conquerors, but these Spanish adventurers wore it like a title of nobility. Cruel they often were, and treacherous; nearly all were greedy for quick fortunes, but their splendid courage blinds us to their faults.

They seem very real and near in the Archives of the Indies. Here are Balboa's own words about "the other sea" he hoped to find. They were written just before he crossed the Isthmus of Panama and actually found the Pacific Ocean. Here are letters from Francisco Pizarro, the Spanish swineherd who conquered the fabulous empire of the Inca Indians in Peru and channeled floods of Inca gold and jewels back to Spain. Here are the records of Ponce de Leon, who set out to find the fountain of youth, and discovered Florida instead. These reports came in from Magellan, the Portuguese navigator who sailed in command of a Spanish expedition of five ships in 1519 and two years later wrote of finding the Philippine Islands. Magellan was killed in the Philippines, but one vessel of his little fleet went on to sail around the world under the Basque navigator, Sebastián del Cano.

These musty documents tell of happenings more marvelous than the plots of any romances of chivalry or of the adventure novels which became the rage during this same age of Conquistadors. They told of knights with elaborate names like Amadís, Florismarte, Palmerín or Don Belianis, who were the Supermen of their day and went about fighting dragons and giants, storming enchanted castles, rescuing beautiful, bewitched ladies from danger and performing other breath-taking feats. We might expect their authors to seize upon the tales brought back by explorers and colonizers as story material, but they preferred to tell and retell, with variations, well-worn fairy tales. Yet no work of fiction compares in excitement and heroism with the true story of how Cortés took Mexico.

Hernán Cortés, a Spanish gentleman-adventurer, lived on his lands in Cuba until he was chosen to lead an expedition exploring territory newly discovered across the Gulf (of Mexico) to the west, whereupon, risking everything on the future, he raised money on his Cuban estates to help pay for the undertaking. Among other preparations he had two banners embroidered in gold with the slogan: "Brothers and companions, let us follow the sign of the Holy Cross with true faith and by it conquer." These banners were flying as he sailed away from Cuba with a force of slightly more than five hundred foot soldiers, a few horsemen and sixteen horses, one hundred sailors, a few small cannons and two hundred Cuban natives and Negroes, who acted as servants and laborers. Upon disembarking in Mexico he caused his ships to be destroyed so there could be no turning back from the enterprise ahead. "Certainly Santiago and our Blessed Lady helped us; put great courage in our hearts," wrote his follower Bernal Díaz, who has left us a brilliant history of the expedition.

Even looking back at it, the conquest of Mexico seems an impossible achievement. Cortés was able to persuade thousands of Indians belonging to tribes subject to the all-powerful Aztec Indians of central Mexico to revolt against these rulers and join his handful of Europeans. Marching north in company with his Indian allies, he seized the sacred person of the Aztec Emperor, Montezuma, and, holding him as a hostage, boldly established himself with his small force in the heart of the teeming Aztec capital, Tenochtitlan (Mexico City). Shortly afterwards, Montezuma was stoned to death by his own people because they thought him a willing captive of the strangers and a traitor to them.

After this murder the aroused Aztecs threatened Cortés and his men with annihilation. The Spanish leader knew they must quit Tenochtitlan at any cost. Under cover of night he led his troops from their quarters in the city, hoping to reach the open country before he was discovered, but the enemy set upon them while they were crossing over a long, narrow causeway which connected the city with the surrounding countryside, attacking with such ferocity that half the Spaniards and thousands of their Indian allies were slaughtered. This night so disastrous to Cortés and his men is called in Mexican history the *Noche triste* or Sad Night. Cortés was among the survivors, and almost immediately after the battle he reassembled the remnants of his forces— wounded, sleepless, hungry men—and counterattacked the hordes of their pursuers. Unbelievable as it seems, the Spaniards won a decisive victory, which assured the conquest of Mexico.

Most Conquistadors thought first of plunder of native gold and jewels—this we must admit. The Spanish rulers, on the other hand, did not consider the Indies merely as a source of treasure. They were anxious to establish colonies there, and while they took the fabulous wealth pouring in from the New World, they sent back to it in return supplies which have produced even greater riches over the centuries. Spanish ships putting into the ports of Seville or Cádiz with cargoes of pearls, emeralds, gold ornaments, gold and silver bullion, exquisite featherwork and native textiles (with llamas, too, from the Andes Mountain regions and bright-feathered birds from the Isthmus of Panama), sailed west again loaded with horses, sheep, cattle, pigs, chickens, dogs—all then unknown in the New World. Plants and seeds went out to flourish in the new soil. Sugar cane, cotton and coffee continued their progress from Arab lands westward. In the Americas, Old World wheat waved beside Indian corn, and fine grapes for wine, transplanted from Spanish vineyards, ripened in the sun.

Spanish colonists often overworked and abused the natives they found living on their land grants. We read of their cruelties—how they forced the Indians to toil on plantations and in mines. In the Caribbean islands, especially, the people were treated so harshly that the Indian race died out, and Negroes were imported to do the hard work.

However, Isabella and her successors on the throne did not advocate or approve such policy. On the contrary, they instructed Spanish authorities in the Indies to treat the Indians "with friendship, so they will come willingly to conversion and knowledge of our holy Catholic faith without any force or maltreatment." No racial barriers were set up between Spaniards and Indians, and laws passed by the royal representatives finally forbade slavery. Years before, when Columbus brought back Indians he intended to sell as slaves, Isabella made him release them. This official attitude of tolerance and kindness towards the natives was more effective than most of us realize. Modern historians generally agree that, in spite of abuses which were bound to occur during conquest and colonization, Spain was more humane than most colonial empires and did less to uproot and destroy the Indians under her rule than any other European country. They point out that nowhere else were savages pacified with so much patience and kindness, nowhere were wide, dangerous frontiers held with so little bloodshed.

The influence of the Catholic Church in the colonies at this time was merciful and wise. Priests and monks who went out to teach and convert, not only defended the Indians against exploitation by the Conquistadors, but they also realized the need for education in the new land, and founded elementary schools everywhere. They established ten or twelve universities, too, among them the University of San Marcos in Lima, Peru, in 1551, and the University of Mexico in 1553. They are nearly a hundred years older than Harvard, our first college in the United States. Churchmen taught, but they also mingled with the Indians as students so as to learn the various native languages. They knew they must be able to preach to the people and teach them in their own tongues. They wrote Spanish-Indian grammars and catechisms and compiled dictionaries. They taught the savages to read and write and the essential facts of Christianity, trained them in useful trades, and showed them improved ways of farming.

Many of these men displayed superb courage and zeal in converting and civilizing the natives; many were as grandly adventurous as the Conquistadors. Two in particular stand out as examples of sixteenth-century Spanish genius—Saint Ignatius Loyola and Saint Francis Xavier.

Ignatius Loyola was a Basque nobleman, handsome, brave, gay and romantic. As a young man, when not fighting or visiting lively, fashionable people, he spent his time reading romances of chivalry. He was thirty when during a battle both his legs were so badly broken by a cannon ball he feared he would be maimed for life. Being vain, he hated the idea of going about as a cripple and had the doctors break the legs and reset them in the hope he would be able to walk better. This meant months of inaction for him—and leisure for reading. Perhaps because he had time to think he grew less vain and frivolous and, putting aside the romances of chivalry, buried himself in religious books. Previously he had dreamed of defending a lovely lady or storming a hill castle; now, still imaginative, he burned to champion the Blessed Virgin Mary, to plant the Catholic faith in every fortress of human belief. He had visions in which he saw Good and Evil as two knights fighting for his soul.

When he could walk again (he limped the rest of his life), instead of returning to his worldly friends, he fasted and studied and saw more visions. One Christmas Eve while praying in the chapel of a monastery, he suddenly felt certain he was the Virgin's squire keeping vigil before being knighted in the morning. Thereafter his mission was clear to him: fight for the Catholic faith. He formed a religious order whose members pledged themselves to obey strict, almost military discipline and fight with heart and mind for Catholic victory. This order was the Society of Jesus, or the Jesuits.

Men from every country in Europe joined the Society of Jesus and went out to minister to every part of the globe. The order grew powerful. Later on, it came to be hated and distrusted in many places, but as it was international rather than purely Spanish in its organization we need not here concern ourselves with its further history. We need only remember that the courage and the dream of conquest (conquest of souls in this case) which created the Jesuits is Spanish and typical of Spain's heroic age.

St. Francis Xavier, the second great religious figure of the sixteenth century, also a Basque nobleman and a Jesuit, was chosen to carry Christianity to India and the Far East. We hear of him among the natives at the southern tip of India baptizing ten thousand heathens; at Goa on the west coast of India, nursing the sick, founding missions and schools, teaching and preaching. In a few years he moved on through the Spice Islands of the South Pacific and from there, three years later, to Japan as its first Christian missionary. Three more years and he set out for China, but he died before reaching the Chinese mainland. His body was returned for burial to Goa, far from the ancient ancestral castle in the north of Spain where he was born.

6. GLITTER—THE HAPSBURGS IN SPAIN

WHILE Spaniards had been exploring and colonizing the Americas, Spain's territory kept growing in Europe. Through successful wars, King Ferdinand added the Kingdom of Naples in southern Italy as well as the Mediterranean islands of Sicily and Sardinia to his lands and then, after Isabella's death, he acquired Navarre, the last independent bit of territory on the Peninsula (except, of course, Portugal) by marrying the heiress to that kingdom, a lady with the pretty name of Germaine de Foix.

When Ferdinand died in 1516, the realms of Castile and Aragon with all their possessions were inherited by a youth of sixteen. This boy was Charles, the grandson of Ferdinand and Isabella. Their own son had died many years before when only nineteen; his loss was unfortunate because he was intelligent and good and because, at his death, his sister Juana became heiress to the throne. Juana was insane. When her husband, Archduke Philip the Handsome of Austria, died she refused to let him be buried, insisting on keeping his body near her always. As she was unfit to reign, her father kept her shut up in a convent and had her son Charles declared heir to the kingdoms of Castile and Aragon.

Far from welcoming their new king, the Spaniards resented him bitterly. To them he was a foreigner, since his father, Archduke Philip, was Austrian, the son of the Hapsburg Emperor Maximilian of Austria. The fact that Charles added to the vast holdings of the Catholic Monarchs the immense domains of his grandfather Maximilian (Austria, parts of Germany, the Netherlands) did not impress his Spanish subjects. He had not been born one of them and this was in their opinion a mark of inferiority; he had not been brought up in Spain, did not, at the beginning of his reign, even speak Spanish well—Spaniards felt he could not live down such handicaps.

For his part, Charles felt small interest in his Spanish realms. At first, he made no move to live in the country, but remained in Austria and Flanders (a section roughly corresponding to modern Belgium and northeastern France), scheming to have himself elected to succeed Maximilian as Holy Roman Emperor. The lay princes of Europe chose one of their number to bear this title and rule them much as the cardinals elected a Pope as their supreme head. In 1519, Charles was indeed elected Holy Roman Emperor. Although the first King Charles of Spain, he was the fifth of his name to rule the Holy Roman Empire, and for this reason is usually spoken of as Charles V, even in Spain.

While maneuvering for imperial honors in the north, Charles had sent Austrian and Flemish nobles to rule Spain. These foreign governors infuriated the Spaniards, who resented the taxes their new King levied to pay his expenses abroad, and loathed the Flemish soldiers he sent into Spain and billeted in Spanish homes. We have some idea of how badly these troops behaved when we recall that under Charles the Spanish word *flamenco* (originally meaning Flemish) changed into a synonym for shameless, vulgar. Finally, bitterness over these abuses flared into revolt throughout northern and central Spain, especially in Castile. This serious uprising has been called the *comuneros,* or revolt of the townsmen, because in general it was the people in the larger cities who took up arms against their King's government, who bore the brunt of the fighting and whose leaders were executed when the rebellion was finally put down. These leaders met death like patriots. One of them, Juan Bravo, cried out just before mounting the scaffold: "We are not traitors, but defenders of the liberty of the realm."

Charles' youth and inexperience must be blamed for the disastrous comuneros. He did not know the Spanish temper—Spanish pride and independence—and he ignored the national passion for local rule.

Everyone in Spain is proudly independent—not just nobles and the rich, but everyone: duke, peasant, bishop and beggar share a deep, inborn self-esteem. Each man feels that being a Spaniard entitles him to consideration from his fellows; he considers he has the right to judge the other man, no matter who he is. Do you recall how the Cid dared confront the King and insult the Pope? Spaniards loved him for this boldness. A Spanish grandee was permitted to wear his hat in the King's presence as a sign of his equality with the sovereign. "We are the King's equals, except we are not so rich," the Castilians used to say. "Each one of us is as good as you and all of us together are better than you," wrote the people of Aragon to their King. Once King Ferdinand said of his soldiers that, fine fighters though they were, their actual disobedience made it almost impossible for a general to control them.

As he grew older, Charles learned to get along better with his Spanish subjects; with passing years, his indifference towards them vanished, and when he was free from war he chose to spend his time in Spain, traveling about, building new palaces and remodeling old ones, presiding at knightly tournaments, fighting bulls in the ring, having his portrait painted. His magnetic personality still colors the Spanish scene; you are shown where he lived and what he built in Madrid, Toledo, Valladolid, Granada, Seville; you are told what he said and did, you sense his grand manner and the glitter of his empire.

And you are often reminded of his military exploits abroad, for war was his chosen profession, one he followed faithfully all his life: He fought four wars with France over Italy, where both nations strove for the controlling influence. He fought the Moorish pirates of North Africa, who had been raiding Spanish shores and seizing Spanish ships—he freed twenty thousand Christians these Moors had been holding as slaves. Early in his reign, his undisciplined army, while in Italy, mutinied, seized Rome and plundered it as though it were an enemy city—which it was not.

The great Protestant reformer, Martin Luther, broke with the Pope and the Catholic Church early in Charles' reign, taking with him as converts to the new faith the rulers and people of numerous German States. Some twenty-five years later, Charles went to war against a coalition of these Lutheran princes, thus beginning the series of religious struggles which replaced in Spanish passions the long fight against the Moors and the long hatred of the Jews.

The strenuous life he led made Charles old before his years. At fifty-five, sensing he had not long to live, he abdicated the throne in favor of his son and heir, Philip II, and retired to the monastery of Yuste, one hundred miles from Madrid, there to spend his last two years in regal splendor, surrounded by a large retinue of courtiers.

Philip II lacked his father's charm and energy, yet he was more popular among the Spanish people than Charles had been, perhaps because he was Spanish born. Those who admire this severe, devout, colorless man say he acted according to his conscience, always seeking the honor and greatness of Spain and the glory of the Spanish Catholic Church according to his understanding of what greatness, honor and glory meant. A visit to the Escorial explains him better than any book could. The Escorial is the large, cold, fortresslike edifice he built on a hillside some thirty miles northwest of Madrid as a palace, a monastery and royal mausoleum. He may have thought the glory of Spain demanded a building as vast as the Escorial (sometimes called the Eighth Wonder of the World) with its more than one hundred miles of narrow corridors, eighty-six staircases, three chapels, fifteen cloisters open to the clear sky, and thousands of windows overlooking the rolling, dun-colored uplands of Castile.

If Philip liked official show and pomp, his personal tastes were simple. His own apartments in the Escorial reflect his piety and severity. The study, where his books still stand on the shelves, is plain as a monk's cell; his bedroom is small and dark; it has an altar in one corner and a window opening above the main church in such a way as to give a full view of the Main Altar. Even when lying ill in bed Philip could look down through the window and follow Mass being celebrated on the Main Altar below.

Philip inherited his father's vast domains except for lands in Germany belonging to the imperial crown (he was not elected Holy Roman Emperor as Charles had been). During his reign he fought and defeated Portugal, joining it to Spain and thus ruling all the Iberian Peninsula. Portugal remained a part of the Spanish Empire for sixty years but regained its independence under Philip IV.

Charles left to his son not only lands but wars and the suspicion and hatred of other European countries, which envied and feared Spain with her great power and her greed for territory. Not having Charles' military bent, Philip seldom accompanied his armies in the field or led them into battle; rather, the pale, slight man sat at his desk hour after hour signing documents, writing out long orders by hand, studying military reports and war plans. How many wars there were! With Portugal and against the Turks, who ruled a great empire from Constantinople, wars with France, with Flanders, military action against the Moors in Granada whom cruel persecution goaded to revolt—even a war against the Pope. All these wars were intended to destroy what was not Spanish and Spanish Catholic.

Two of the best-known battles in history occurred during Philip II's reign, both sea fights: the Battle of Lepanto and the defeat of the Spanish Armada.

In the first, Spain allied herself with Venice and the Pope against the Turks, and fought them in the Strait of Lepanto off the western coast of Greece. Philip's dashing half brother, Don Juan of Austria, commanded the allied fleet in a stunning victory. Do you recall Gilbert Chesterton's poem about Lepanto with the line "Don John of Austria is going to the war" throbbing through? Who can forget this picture of victory?

> Don John of Austria has burst the battle line!
> Don John pounding from the slaughter-painted poop,
> Purpling all the ocean like a bloody pirate's sloop,
> Scarlet running over on the silvers and the golds . . .
> Breaking of the hatches up and bursting of the holds. . . .

The Armada expedition was disastrous for Spain. Wishing to crush the sea power of England and thus cut off the help she was giving his rebellious Protestant subjects in the Netherlands, Philip assembled the greatest fleet or armada of the age, 132 ships and thirty thousand men. Unfortunately, the great admiral who organized the expedition and was to lead it died just before sailing time. The courtier Philip chose to succeed him knew nothing at all about the sea or sea fighting and told the King how incompetent he felt himself to be. However, Philip was so certain of victory he insisted this gentleman take command anyway, saying that the Lord would be the true Admiral of the Fleet.

It seemed as though the Lord were the true Admiral of the English Fleet, not the Spanish. From the beginning, misfortune dogged the Spaniards. As the fleet rounded the northwestern tip of Spain, gales scattered the ships, crippled some and sank others. In the English Channel off Plymouth and, later, off Calais, the swifter British vessels with their long-range guns worked destruction on the clumsy, many-decked Spanish galleons and the little galleys. The Spaniards could not maneuver close enough to the English vessels to board them for the hand-to-hand fighting on which they had counted. The *Bull,* the *Bear,* the *Black Dog,* the *Revenge* harried and sank or drove to the north such once-proud ships as *Santa María, San Marcos, San Luís, San Mateo* and countless others.

"Jehovah blew and they were scattered," exulted the English as gales and bad weather continued to haunt the North Sea, where nineteen more Spanish vessels went down. At last, after weeks of hunger, fever and scurvy, of more storms and other hardships, about half the original Armada limped back to Spanish ports. They tell of one of its admirals who brought a few ships he had managed to protect into San Sebastián. When he landed he looked at no one, spoke to no one, not even his wife and children, and going home, locked himself in his room to lie with his face to the wall and die.

King Philip was more resigned. On receiving the dreadful news he said quietly: "I did not expect that my fleet would have to fight the weather."

Spain's title to mastery in Europe went down that stormy summer of 1588 with the Armada's defeat. Well before Philip's death, ten years later, his empire had begun to crack and fall apart. It continued to break away little by little from his successors.

Philip II died in 1598, as the century was ending. Three more Hapsburg kings divided the seventeenth century among their reigns, Philip II's son, Philip III, his grandson, Philip IV and his great-grandson, Charles II, a poor feeble-minded fellow who believed that devils had taken possession of his soul and body.

Philip III signed the decree expelling the Moriscos, Moors remaining in Spain after the fall of Granada, who had been forced to become Christians. The Moriscos had done the hard work most Spaniards scorned; they were masons, shoemakers, carpenters, tailors, weavers in every community, as well as the best farmers. Although they were a a patient people, they rebelled against enforced conversion and destruction of their old culture, the burning of their precious books and ruin of their beautiful buildings. Their rebellions were frequent and serious until at last, in 1609, Philip III ordered them out of the country within three days. Between half a million and nine hundred thousand men, women and children were hustled out of Spain to North Africa and other Mediterranean places. The authorities permitted a very few, about six per cent of the total number, to remain in Spain and carry on Moorish methods of farming and irrigation. Later on, many exiles braved punishment and crept back to their old homes.

Spain suffered from their loss for no one was willing to do the drab, everyday work they had performed; Spaniards themselves were too busy dreaming of gold and adventure overseas. Moreover, the brave and capable among them, carrying through such dreams, were emigrating by thousands to the New World in search of fortune, while other thousands were serving with Spanish armies in Flanders, France and Italy. The idle and no-account left at home began drifting to the big cities.

Economic conditions in Spain during the seventeenth century grew steadily worse; you saw poverty everywhere. The middle classes were in dire need of the necessities of life while the poor often starved to death. Hunger is a favorite theme with authors of the period. A

Spaniard wrote this description of conditions at the time:

Traverse the fields once fertile; you will see them covered with nettles and briars; for there is no longer anyone who cultivates them. The largest part of the Spaniards do nothing today, some under the pretext of nobility, others because they prefer to beg. The streets of Madrid offer a singular spectacle. They are encumbered with do-nothings and vagabonds who pass their days in playing cards, in waiting for the hour to dine at the gate of convents or to set out for the country to loot houses. What is worse, not only has this life of idleness been adopted, but the plazas swarm with adventurers and vagabonds whose vices corrupt all the town and people the hospitals.

The idleness of the people was a result as well as one of the causes of the depression in Spain. Another reason for the nation's financial troubles lay in senseless restrictions put on trade and industry. Foolish regulations hampered the manufacture of goods for which the country was famous in Europe and caused the loss of foreign markets. For instance, a shoemaker was punished if he did not obey exact rules as to the style and type of shoe he might make. No fine silks or woolens might be exported to the Americas—but only the coarsest cloth. Trade with the Spanish colonies in the Americas did not bring in the revenues it should have. For one reason, it was restricted to a few individuals and all of it trickled through a single port, at first Seville and later Cádiz. The colonies were forbidden to trade with any country except Spain, and yet Spain would not send them clothes, farm implements, or tools. The English, Dutch and French did a flourishing contraband in such articles, smuggling them in to settlers who needed them and were willing and able to pay for what they bought. These three nations also grew rich on the capture at sea of Spanish ships laden with fortunes in American gold and silver.

Although taxes on the people grew heavier with every year, the kings, beginning with Charles V, never had enough money to pay for their wars or the elaborate court life. Most of the time Philip III neglected to pay his servants; Philip IV set up boxes in the churches begging his subjects to drop into them contributions towards his personal expenses; feeble-minded Charles II let the horses in the royal

stables starve to death because he felt he could not afford to feed
them. Yet when Philip IV's daughter went off to marry King Louis
XIV of France, she needed seventy horses to carry her silver and perfumes; packed her dresses in twenty satin-covered, silver-bound trunks
and her gloves in two satin trunks bound with gold!

7. THE GOLDEN AGE

WHEN we speak of the sixteenth and seventeenth centuries in
Spain as the Golden Age, we are not thinking of Spanish power and
material treasures but rather of the wealth of Spanish literature and
art, the rich flowering of Spanish genius. During this period, Spanish
writers and painters created works which have been delighting the
world ever since.

One treasure was a new literary form, the picaresque novel, so-called
because its hero is a *pícaro* or rogue, in which Spanish writers
turned the poverty and sordid life they saw about them into an adventure tale. But not an adventure tale like the romance of chivalry. In
the romance of chivalry the knight met dragons and fell into an enchanted sleep in castle or deep woodland, won a dukedom and a beautiful lady; in the picaresque novel, the rogue associated with murderers
and pickpockets, slept in gutters and filthy hovels, stole a loaf of bread
or a few coins when hungry, met only servant girls, shrewish inkeep-
ers' wives or drunken old women. The hero of the romance of chivalry
succeeded through his fantastic bravery; the pícaro lived by his wits.
The action of the romance of chivalry whirled in cloudy worlds of
romance; the picaresque novels limped along through real life, showing candid-camera shots of the hard, vicious, often happy-go-lucky
vagrants and criminals who thronged city streets and made country

roads dangerous for travelers. They told the same story of crime and poverty and suffering that can be read in records of the time—but more amusingly.

The first picaresque novel and a famous one is *Lazarillo de Tormes,* which was published in 1554. Told in the first person, supposedly by Lazarillo, the hero, it takes us on his various adventures. When his rascally father dies fighting the Moors in North Africa, his mother finds it so hard to feed her child that she "hires" him out to a blind beggar. This old fellow knows more than a hundred prayers to be recited for special occasions and intentions and collects plenty of food and money, but he is so miserly that Lazarillo would starve if he did not steal bread from the blind man's provision bag, wine from his jug and a few pennies now and then. When his master catches Lazarillo draining his wine he breaks the jug in the boy's face, then wipes off the cuts made by the broken pottery with a rag soaked in the spilled wine. Lazarillo hates him for this and other cruelties and takes revenge by leading the old fellow over the roughest roads he can find. "If there were stones, through them, if mud into the deepest of it."

Leaving the beggar, he serves a priest, but, as he says, he escapes from the thunder to run into the lightning, for the priest, too, is a miser. Lazarillo starves on a diet of onions, thin meat broth and gnawed bones until he steals the key to a chest where his master hoards bread. When the food is missed Lazarillo says rats and snakes have been robbing the chest. At last, however, the priest catches him in his thievery and puts him out of the house. He serves others, among them a well-dressed, penniless, hungry gentleman who is too proud to work. There is a monk among his masters, and a constable; with them all Lazarillo lives by his wits, not too well at that.

The Spanish picaresque novel set a literary style in Europe; it was copied in England, France, Germany, Holland. Even our own Tom Sawyer and Huck Finn have some pícaro ink in their veins.

Pícaros and the rascally society about them have never been better depicted than in the short stories of Miguel de Cervantes, a Golden Age author whom we remember for his masterpiece, *Don Quixote.*

Critics, however, say his short stories would have made Cervantes famous had he never written *Don Quixote*. One, "Rinconete and Cortadillo," is about two boys, one a pickpocket and the other a cardsharper, who join a rogues' union in Seville and meet many other rascals. The tale is wonderfully realistic; it makes you feel the heat, smell and see the filth, hear the laughter and curses echoing down the docks along the Guadalquivir River; it leads you right into the small, bare room where the rogues hold their meeting.

Cervantes wrote from actual experience of the low life of Seville, for he must have met just such characters as those he described while he was in jail in Seville or Valladolid. In Seville he was imprisoned for poor management of government funds. He had never been accused of using any of the "lost" money for himself—he simply seems to have had no head for business. In Valladolid he was taken to jail following the death of a man he did not even know, who had been set upon and murdered outside the miserable lodgings where the Cervantes family were living. Cervantes rubbed against the rough edges of life; had he been unscrupulous he might have lived out a real pícaro story.

He had an adventurous youth: To Naples in his early twenties in the suite of a young cardinal, enlistment in a Spanish regiment recruited there for war against the Turkish pirates, the battle of Lepanto. When the Christian and Turkish fleets joined for this battle he was sick with fever but insisted on taking up arms, for, he said, what would people say if he did not do his duty; he would rather die fighting for God and King than remain below decks. He was wounded three times during the fighting, one shot ruining his left hand.

Recovering from his wounds, he saw more military service and then sailed for Spain in hopes of a government job as a reward for valor. In sight of the Spanish coast, Algerian pirates boarded the ship, killed the captain and many sailors and passengers and took the survivors, Cervantes among them, to Algiers, where they were sold as slaves. He was a captive there for five and half years, often in chains because of four attempts he made to escape. Finally, a monk whose lifework was collecting money to free Christians from captivity ransomed him just as his owner was preparing to move to Constantinople; Cervantes already lay in chains in the hold of the ship on which they were to travel.

From here on he is hard to follow for his life over the next forty years was poor and obscure. He wrote plays but they were not successful; he wrote a novel about shepherds and shepherdesses in the literary style of the age, but it was dull; he could not make a living from poetry although now and then he won a poetry prize. He married and had a daughter; his sisters, poor also, lived in his household. He worked for the government getting supplies for the army during the time of preparation for the Armada. He tried for four different jobs overseas but without success. Sometimes we lose sight of him for several years until his name appears in some legal document or other.

At fifty-eight, he published the first part of *Don Quixote;* at sixty-eight, the year before his death, he finished the second part of the novel which more than one critic has called the world's greatest. Beyond doubt it has been the most popular over the centuries, having gone into more editions and foreign translations than any other work except the Bible. Shelf upon shelf of books discuss it. Philosophers, critics and poets have amused themselves trying to define the exact meaning of every line, to find a lesson in every mad adventure of its hero, the elderly knight from a village in the region of La Mancha.

Suppose we think of *Don Quixote* as a romance of chivalry set in the real world.

Don Quixote himself walks out of the first page of the book named for him; you know him at once, this gentleman with the thin horse and a hunting dog, who lives in his family house with his niece and a housekeeper, so poor that he has to spend three fourths of his income for food and the rest for clothes. With too much time on his hands, he turns to romances of chivalry and becomes such a bookworm he forgets to go hunting or to attend to his small estate. "From reading so much and sleeping so little, his brains dried up." He feels he must go out and be a knight-errant like the heroes in the novels, and, since he is quite mad, is sure he can right the wrongs of the world.

He cleans up his grandfather's armor, which has rusted in the attic; when he finds no helmet up there—only a soldier's headpiece shaped like a lady's narrow-brimmed hat—he makes a cardboard vizor and pastes it to the hat. Then he tries out his helmet, but his sword pierces the cardboard and he has to make another vizor. This second helmet he is careful not to test out for fear of damaging before his adventures begin. He gives his old nag the fancy name of Rosinante, which, despite the fine sound, means a miserable work horse.

Since every knight adores some lady and performs brave deeds for her, our hero must have one, too: for he thinks a knight-errant who is not in love is like a tree without leaves and fruit, or a body without its soul. He has long secretly admired a good-looking, husky farm girl of the neighborhood who scarcely knows he exists. She shall be his lady. Her name, Aldonaza Lorenzo, is not romantic enough for a knight's beloved, so he calls her Dulcinea del Toboso and swears eternal devotion to her.

Let us follow him on one of his marvelous adventures:

After he has had himself (he thinks) dubbed a knight by the landlord of a wretched inn (whom he takes for the lord of a castle), he realizes that every knight needs a squire. So he rides home to his village and persuades a fat country neighbor, one Sancho Panza, to leave wife and children and ride forth with him. Sancho, though sane and usually governed by common sense, is so fascinated by the prospect of knight-errantry along the roads and in the mountains and fields that he mounts his donkey and comes willingly, dreaming of rich booty he will collect from his lord's conquests. He never doubts his lord for long, even though his eyes may recognize windmills where Don Quixote, seeing evil giants, charges into the turning blades of one, only to be painfully thrown.

Sancho knows a flock of sheep, too, even though his master insists they are really an army approaching. In fact, Sancho points out that two flocks of sheep are converging on the spot where they have halted; nevertheless, he asks humbly: "What are we to do, señor?" "Do," cries Don Quixote. "We must aid the needy and weak. Know, Sancho, that the army approaching ahead of us is led and guided by the mighty Emperor Alifanfarón, Lord of the great island of Trapobana. This other behind us is that of his enemy, the King of the Garamantas, Pentapolín of the Uplifted Arm, who always goes into battle with his right arm bare."

"Why don't these gentlemen like each other?" asks Sancho.

"They dislike each other," replies Don Quixote, "because this Alifanfarón, a raving pagan, is madly in love with the daughter of Pentapolín, a beautiful and charming lady, and she is a Christian and her father does not want to give her to a pagan king unless he first abandons the faith of his false prophet Mohammed and turns to ours."

"By my beard," cries Sancho, carried away and disbelieving his eyes, "Pentapolín is doing right and I must help him as much as I can."

Knight and squire ride to the gentle slope of a hill from which, as they watch the onswirling clouds of dust, Don Quixote continues to name illustrious knights and nobles riding through the haze—their shields, banners, distinctive armor. Poor, puzzled Sancho admits he cannot see one of them. "It must be enchantment," he says. However, when Don Quixote charges into the flock of sheep, Sancho remains on the slope. After his master has killed several sheep and the shepherds, having nearly killed his master with showers of stones, have hurried from the spot, Sancho goes to the injured knight. "Didn't I tell you, you were going to charge into sheep?" he scolds.

It is too bad we cannot keep on following the pair over the dusty roads, through mountain thickets and into dirty Spanish inns of the day, seeing, like Sancho Panza, the reality before us, yet, like him, half convinced that reality is not so true as Don Quixote's mad vision.

Cervantes' fame is international, for Don Quixote seems to belong to us all. Lope de Vega, on the other hand, though a genius as unusual as Cervantes, is so peculiarly Spanish that his name is much better known than his works. It has been said, too, that if he had written half as much, he would be twice as famous, for a literary critic hesitates to form opinions about an author whose existing works include 475 full-length plays known to be genuine, 53 others thought to be so, besides 50 one-act religious dramas, called *autos* and thousands of pages of prose novels, history and long narrative poems.

Lope was unquestionably the most prolific writer the world has known. In his long life he produced eighteen hundred full-length plays of all types—tragedy, comedy and the *comedia de capa y espada* (cloak and sword play), which is one long intrigue of mistaken identities, disguises and surprises. He often turned out a play in two days, writing in longhand without the help of any secretary or assistant. When he sailed with the Armada, he put in his spare time aboard ship writing a long narrative poem in eleven cantos. He went to many sources for his plots—Bible stories, lives of the saints, Spanish legends, romances of chivalry, the wars in Italy, the Netherlands and Algiers, the struggle with the Moors for Granada. His pictures of everyday life seem almost in Cinemascope and Technicolor, they are so clear and true. His verses, which lose by translation, are velvety, bright, charming. His ideas bubble and foam and overflow; they are romantic, patriotic, witty, sarcastic and sometimes very sensible—like these lines from a cloak and sword comedy:

> The use of speech is taught
> To men and birds alike, but silence yet
> It never has been taught. And what a pity!
> It is a great mistake to open schools
> To teach us how to talk and not have one
> That can teach us to be still.
> *(A Certainty for a Doubt,* Act I)*

While none of Lope's plays have been acted in English, some are translated into our language as well as into French, German, Russian, Polish, Yiddish. They have been often given on European stages, and frequently since 1939 you see them, as well as the work of Lope's contemporaries, in Spanish theaters.

There were other great Spanish dramatists in the Golden Age, among them Pedro Calderón de la Barca, who is better known abroad than Lope. Several English poets have translated passages of his brilliant

---

* Translated by John Garrett Underhill in *Four Plays of Lope de Vega.* Charles Scribner's Sons, New York. By permission.

poetry. You often hear of his *Mágico prodigioso* (The Marvelous Magician), and *La Vida es sueño* (Life Is a Dream). In the first drama, a pagan scholar who sells his soul to the devil is saved by the young Christian girl he loves, becomes a Christian and with her suffers martyrdom. *Life Is a Dream* tells of a prince imprisoned from infancy in a lonely tower by order of his father, the King, because astrologers foretold he would be wicked and destructive. When the father brings the unhappy prince to court to test the truth or falsehood of these predictions, the young man is transported while in a drugged sleep. Awaking, he is told that memories of his former life are only bad dreams. When he behaves in a savage and arrogant way, he is again drugged and returned to his tower prison where his keeper insists that the court experiences were the dream. In the end, restored to his father and the court, he is a wiser and gentler man.

Compared to Lope, Calderón did not write much—only about 120 plays, numerous *autos* and the first *zarzuelas*, which are short comedies with singing and dancing, usually based on old folk music. The zarzuela has been popular in Spain ever since Calderón's time; now, however, it is beginning to change—it contains less folk music and many more modern rhythms.

A third playwright of the period, Tirso de Molino, wrote three or four hundred plays; we recall him for one in particular, *El Burlador de Sevilla* (The Gay Deceiver of Seville), which introduces to the world Don Juan, the great lover, the brave, unprincipled and heartless heartbreaker. As you know, French, Italian, English and Austrian composers and writers have "borrowed" Don Juan. He has continued to charm Spaniards, too, since Tirso. A little over a hundred years ago, a Spanish author, José Zorrilla, made him the hero of his play *Don Juan Tenorio*. In Zorrilla's drama, Don Juan is saved from hell, to which his sins condemn him, by the love of Doña Inés, a pure young girl. The play is so popular among Spanish-speaking people that it has been given every year for more than a century in theaters in Spain and Latin America during the first days of November, around All Souls' Day, when Catholics say special prayers for their dead.

The Golden Age was rich not only in writers; its painters, too, were numerous and some have become world-famous. Three of the greatest, with whose canvases most of us are familiar, are El Greco, Velásquez and Murillo.

El Greco's real name was Domenicos Theotocopoulos, but they called him The Greek for short because he had been born on Crete, a Greek island. After study in Italy with great artists, he came to Spain in 1575 and settled in Toledo, there to pass the remaining forty years of his life. After seeing one of his paintings, you cannot fail to recognize the others, for all are in the unmistakable style of his strange genius— long, narrow faces and long, twisted figures in the portraits; somber, unearthly colors, a sense of foreboding hanging over the landscapes like a thunderstorm about to break. We have numerous El Greco canvases in the United States, one of the most famous being his vision of Toledo, which is in the Metropolitan Museum in New York City. The painter does not see Toledo as the city of warm browns and terra cottas it is, but rather as a place of unearthly greens, with sick, greenish-white buildings and fortifications slipping down through decaying greens of the landscape, under a black-green, blue-green mottled sky to the slimy underwater green of the river. Having once viewed Toledo in El Greco's painting, you never forget his vision of the city.

The Prado in Madrid has a wealth of art from many countries and ages, yet almost certainly on your first visit you will be dazzled by the work of one painter—Velásquez, the bulk of whose output—some fifty paintings—is collected there. Velásquez has perpetuated the court of King Philip IV more royally than artist has ever done for any other king. There are seven portraits of Philip himself, several charming ones of Don Baltasar Carlos, Philip's handsome eldest son who died at sixteen, numerous pictures of his daughter, Margarita Teresa and portraits of other members of the royal family and courtiers; wonderfully sympathetic paintings, too, of the court dwarfs. No artist surpasses Velásquez in drawing, in color, in the magic of light and shadow; no one has looked about with clearer eyes or transferred what he saw to canvas with surer hand.

His masterpiece, *Las Meninas* (The Maids of Honor), hangs in a room to itself. A large mirror on the wall opposite the painting reflects the scene just as the artist must have viewed it in a mirror as he painted. He himself is in the picture, too, on the left facing you as you stand looking at it. There is enchantment in this maze of mirrors, real and painted, and you feel like Alice slipping through the looking glass into another world, the court of Philip IV. Before you stands the fair-haired little princess, Margarita Teresa; she seems so alive you wonder if she brushed past you a moment ago in her white satin, grown-up dress. You watch her graceful maids of honor, marvel at the two ugly dwarfs, like her big, sleepy dog. Light from a window at your right touches the faces of the princess and her attendants; light streams in through an open door at the far end of the spacious studio; elsewhere, shadows scatter silver dust through the room. King Philip and his wife, Queen Mariana, dimly reflected in a mirror against the back wall of the picture room, appear to be standing just beside you for the mirror to have caught them so. You half expect to see your own image reflected with theirs.

Both Velásquez and Murillo were born and brought up in Seville, but Velásquez was eighteen years older and had risen to be court painter by the time his young fellow townsman came to Madrid, poor and unknown. He befriended Murillo in many ways, but did not influence his style. Velásquez made people of this world live in the world; Murillo's Virgins and angels, cherubs and saints are human beings too, but he gives them such sweetness and gayety that they seem unearthly. You may have seen his charming Blessed Virgins floating up to heaven accompanied by admiring cherubs. About forty Murillos hang in the Prado, but Seville is his city, and he is Seville's favorite painter. You find many of his canvases there, in the cathedral and other churches and buildings; you visit his house on a little plaza of the old quarter. When you find a Murillo which does not treat a religious subject, it suggests Seville to you—the ragged boys eating melons and grapes or bread might be urchins he watched in some pícaro-infested neighborhood near the river. As you walk, even today, through some narrow street in Seville with late afternoon turning shadows to the browns and gray-golds Murillo liked to paint, you half expect, looking up to some window, to meet the merry, impish glance of one of the dark-eyed young girls he portrayed with such freshness and grace.

8. TARNISH—THE INQUISITION

YOU have all heard of the Spanish Inquisition. It was a tribunal of the Catholic Church which Ferdinand and Isabella established in Spain (with the reluctant permission of the Pope) for the trial and sentencing of anyone whose beliefs or behavior did not conform to the strict pattern of the religion of the state. There had existed a so-called Inquisition in Europe since the thirteenth century, but the Spanish Inquisition was more active and harsher in its judgments than any before it. It was a national project for Spain, with Queen Isabella seeing it as a way to keep Catholics true to the Church, and Ferdinand thinking of it as a powerful political weapon. In those days, the ruler controlled the Church in Spain, and an enemy of his government could therefore be considered an enemy of the Church and brought before the Inquisition for punishment.

Ferdinand and Isabella and high churchmen close to them may have considered the Inquisition a fine way to save souls and keep Spain a strong, united nation, but the country as a whole did not share their enthusiasm for it. When Ferdinand ordered his subjects in Aragon, Valencia and Catalonia to receive the Inquisitors and help them establish the court, they refused—the clergy as well as laymen. Catalonia, especially, objected, and wrangled for three years with Ferdinand before letting him organize the Inquisition in the city of Barcelona.

The Inquisition, which has written the darkest pages in Spanish history, can not be defended, but we do explain it to a certain extent by thinking of it as the longest and most severe case of an epidemic of the times. Spain and Roman Catholicism were not alone in their cruelty and intolerance, for injustices also infected other religions and countries of Europe. Lutherans, as well as Catholics, in Germany persecuted Protestant sects like the Moravians and Dunkards, many of whose members fled to freedom in the United States. In Switzerland, the famous Protestant leader, John Calvin, burned for heresy the Spanish physician Miguel Serveto (or Servet), who is credited with discovering the circulation of the blood. Catholics and Protestants alike died for their faith in France and England.

The Inquisition adopted a green cross as its symbol and all Spain cringed at sight of it. People from every class of society had to face the dreaded body—churchmen who disagreed with details of dogma, converted Jews whose sincerity was questioned, hysterical men and women claiming visions and the power of prophecy, British and Dutch sailors from ships captured raiding on the high seas or plundering the coasts of the Americas. Now and then it tried writers and painters, though not a single author or artist is known to have been sentenced to death by it. It had no jurisdiction over natives of the Indies and paid no attention to the gypsies roaming the Peninsula, although they scoffed at religion and lived openly disgraceful lives.

All types of law courts in Europe during the fifteenth, sixteenth and seventeenth centuries customarily used torture to extract confessions from persons accused of crimes, and the Inquisition followed this practice, with no more brutality than other courts. However, such procedure seems unchristian and shocking in a religious tribunal. The powers of the Inquisition were boundless. It could order the arrest of a man, keep him in prison for months or even years before bringing him to trial and need not inform him of what he was accused or by whom, until the trial. He was, however, permitted to make out a list of his enemies and the testimony of anyone on such a list was not used against him. The trial, when finally held, was secret. If a prisoner refused to confess the crime alleged against him, torture often forced

The Roman aqueduct at Segovia

Castilian landscape near Jadraque, New Castile

Looking down the broad Calle de Alcalá in Madrid

Renaissance architecture, courtyard in
the cathedral at Santiago de Compostela

A *paso* bearing a statue of the Virgin in the Holy Week procession at Seville. *Photograph by Antonio Roldan.*

Melons ripening on the roof of a
shrine in a Galician fishing village

Peaks of the Pyrenees near Santander

The escutcheoned doorway of a house in Jerez de la Frontera

Moorish garden in Málaga

The Cathedral of Seville showing La Giralda

Sheep raising and wool weaving are major industries in Old Castile

The Cathedral of Salamanca

The port of Vigo in Galicia

Primitive threshing on a farm near Burgos

Young people arriving at the April *Feria* in Seville

Street scene in Orense, Galicia

him to change his testimony. He was supposed to repeat this confession when free of torture; if he would not do so, he might be put to the torture again—and again—and again.

In the end, he might possibly be cleared and released; perhaps he was sentenced to nothing worse than a pilgrimage to some shrine in penance for his sins; or, he might be compelled to wear a yellow tunic with a red cross, signifying that he had sinned but was repentant. Sometimes he went to prison for six months, for a year, ten years, the rest of his life. If the sentence of death was pronounced against him, the Church authorities turned him over to the civil government, which executed the decree.

The official act of sentencing and punishing a prisoner of the Inquisition was called an *auto de fe* (act of faith), and was conducted with much ceremony. It drew many spectators, who seemed to consider it as thrilling a drama as they could possibly watch. In the fifteenth and sixteenth centuries, the people flocked by thousands to the main square of town or city to see the Inquisitors arrive in solemn procession, to watch the accused led in and to hear the verdict read out. This was the first act of the drama; the second act, or execution of the sentence, usually took place the following day, again before an interested throng of onlookers. King Philip II often was present at such affairs. We read of his attending one *auto de fe* in Valladolid when eighteen persons were burned for heresy; another time, on a fine June day in the city of Toledo, he brought his children to witness the condemnation of a man to one hundred lashes and one year's imprisonment for claiming to have trances and the ability to prophesy. Torture, misery and death have always fascinated the Spaniards, as we so clearly perceive in their art, literature and history; the Spanish genius for enduring hardships and the Spaniard's almost unconquerable courage are also expressed in indifference to pain and a lack of pity for suffering.

The name of the first Grand Inquisitor (Chief Judge) has become a synonym for intolerance and cruelty. Once this man, Tomás de Torquemada, caused six thousand "suspicious or heretical" books to be burned in a single day in Seville. During eighteen years as Grand Inquisitor, he judged over a hundred thousand accused persons. Historians dispute over how many he condemned to death; some say no more than ninety, others claim four thousand, while still others put the figures as high as nine thousand. This confusion may be due to the fact that many of those about to be arrested and brought before the Inquisition were warned in time to escape from Spain. Even though absent, they were tried; if condemned to death, they were burnt in effigy.

Although the Inquisition did not end legally in Spain until 1834, it had dwindled to a shadow of its terrible self long before then; indeed, its power was gone by the end of the seventeenth century and we hear of it only very occasionally after that.

9. FRENCH ENAMEL—THE BOURBONS

WHEN Charles II, the last of the Hapsburg line of kings in Spain, died in 1700, a new dynasty—the Bourbons—took over the country. The first King of this family was Philip V, whose Bourbon grandfather was King Louis XIV of France. Poor, feeble-minded Charles II had no direct heir and so willed his crown to Philip. Philip's claim came through his Spanish grandmother—you may remember the elaborate trousseau the young lady took with her when she went off to France to be married. However, another prince also claimed the throne, the Archduke Charles of Austria, a Hapsburg and closely connected with the family that had ruled Spain for nearly two hundred years.

When Philip V became King of Spain at the age of seventeen, he found himself at war with Archduke Charles and his supporters—England, Austria, Holland and the Spanish province of Catalonia.

France, of course, took Philip's side. The struggle was a costly one; when it ended, Philip kept the crown but Spain had lost valuable territories in Europe, and, most humiliating of all, England held Gibraltar, that precious bit of Spanish rock. She has kept it ever since, to the deep wounding of Spanish pride. Catalonia made peace with King Philip but he took away its ancient rights to self-government and banned the public use of the Catalan language.

Philip V was an improvement over such Hapsburgs as Philip IV and Charles II because he brought some order out of the financial chaos he found. He also improved conditions by building bridges and good roads—the old ones being little better than trails—by cleaning up Madrid, until then a muddy, filthy place, and by constructing numerous handsome buildings, among others the Royal Palace in Madrid and the lovely castle of La Granja a few miles from the city of Segovia. Disturbed by lawless hordes of vagrants infesting the cities, he ordered all men fit for military service into the army and sent the others, the sick and old, to hospitals and poorhouses.

If we compare the castle of La Granja with the somber Escorial built by Philip II we understand the great change which had come to Spain's rulers with the advent of Philip V. La Granja some seventy miles northwest of Madrid, is built in the French manner and resembles the Palace of Versailles near Paris. Some people think it more beautiful than Versailles because the gardens of Versailles lie in a level landscape, whereas the smooth green lawns, clipped hedges, leafy walks, avenues of statues and elaborate fountains of La Granja look up from their careful beauty to the wild peaks of the Guadarrama Mountains, snow-covered even in early summer.

The Escorial, for all its magnificence, is harsh and tomblike; La Granja has a gay and worldly air. Each palace is typical of its royal builder. Philip V did not share Philip II's obsessions with death and eternity or his warlike religious fervor. Philip V, being less bigoted than his predecessors, took away some of the Inquisition's powers; he revived schools and universities which had been almost stifled by strict censorship. Once again, Spaniards were allowed to go abroad for study; once more, French and other foreign books were brought into the country. Worldly Spaniards mingled with foreign wits and scholars at the royal court. Nevertheless, these new, more liberal ideas did not affect the great mass of the people, who kept to their old ways and their old superstitions.

We might compare the eighteenth century in Spain to a fine French enamel laid over the iron of Spanish temperament. Smooth, talented writers and painters and architects adorned the period, and yet only one true Spanish genius burst through the artificial glaze of French artistic fashion with passionate flame. Towards the end of the century, Francisco Goya, the painter, expressed perfectly the Spaniard's tragic, comic, intense feeling for life.

Although Philip V and his two sons, who reigned after him, had tidied up the economic clutter in Spain, their policy abroad soon brought on new disorder, for they kept the nation at war during most of the eighteenth century—with England, Austria, Holland and Portugal. Before the period ended, Spain had lost all her European empire except the Balearics and the Canary Islands.

The nineteenth century, which found Philip's grandson, Charles IV, on the throne, proved even more ruinous and disgraceful than the preceding one. It dawned under the shadow of Napoleon Bonaparte with his greed for world rule. Instead of ordering Napoleon to keep north of the Pyrenees, both Charles and his son Ferdinand intrigued and plotted with him until he outwitted them and seized Spain for himself. The whole affair is one of greed, stupidity and wickedness; if you think of it as an absorbing story, then Goya's portraits of the principal characters in the plot (all except Napoleon himself) make wonderful illustrations. Look at King Charles IV in the many portraits by Goya which hang in the Prado in Madrid. How vulgar and stupid he is—vain, too, with his jeweled decorations spread across his fat body. Look at his queen, María Luisa, her beady eyes staring out from under a thicket of hair. Napoleon said her character was written in her face and that it was incredible. Even as a young boy, their son Ferdinand has a mean, sly face. At first the Spaniards called Ferdinand *El Deseado* (The Desired), but that title degenerated into sarcasm, for no people could desire such a contemptible ruler. Finally, there are Goya's portraits of Godoy, the Queen's favorite, coarsely handsome and ambitious but not clever enough to prove even a fair prime minister. Compare these people with the personages you saw in the Velásquez paintings of Philip IV and his family: the King, Queen Mariana, the royal children and the courtiers are dignified and gravely elegant, whereas this later royal family seems merely vulgar and cheap.

Cheap and vulgar they were, as well as stupid. Each thought only of himself and plotted and counterplotted. In the end, caught in Napoleon's net, the King and Queen went into exile for life, as did Godoy, while Ferdinand spent five years as a virtual prisoner in a French castle during the time that Napoleon's brother Joseph balanced on the shaky throne of Spain. When the Spaniards were not calling Joseph worse names, they spoke of him as *Pepe Botellas,* or Joe Bottles, because he drank so much wine.

By the time Napoleon had lured Charles, Ferdinand and Godoy across the border into France, about seventy thousand French troops were already in Spain. On May 2, 1808, word spread through Madrid that Napoleon had ordered those members of the royal family still in Madrid to be brought to France. Hearing that Don Francisco, one of the royal princes, a boy of thirteen, did not want to leave Madrid and had been crying bitterly at the thought of exile, the people gathered about the carriage in which he was to travel and, in an explosion of anger, cut the traces and led the horses away. At this, French troops charged the crowds, firing on them with cannons and rifles. The Madrileños fought back with sticks and stones and knives. Later, a Spanish officer gave them arms from a nearby garrison and they fought with guns. In the end, however, the trained French soldiers put down the riot. Its ringleaders, and many others besides, were immediately shot. However, a new war, another Reconquest had begun that day and *el dos de mayo* (May second) rallied the patriots as Covadonga once had.

In the Prado, you see Goya's paintings of the horror and suspense, the brutality of French executions during *el dos de mayo*. Goya and his gardener stole out after the fighting ended that night, he with a rifle and sketching pad. Whenever the moon broke through the clouds, he put down the gun to sketch the faces and attitudes of the dead, lying unburied in the city streets and open fields.

This second Reconquest fell to the Spanish people. They had no king to lead them, few members of the aristocracy among them; they were without money for war supplies; at first, the few regular army troops siding with them were defeated. Most of the fighting men were volunteers who used hit-run tactics—guerrilla warfare in the country which coined the word (*guerrilla* means "little war"). They harried Napoleon's veterans in this way until, at the battle of Bailén in the south of Spain, they met and defeated twenty-two thousand well-trained French troops.

The Spaniards are proud of Bailén; they also boast of the glory and horror of the sieges of Zaragoza and Gerona. That the unfortified city of Zaragoza on its tawny plain beside the Ebro River withstood two separate, two-month sieges remains a mystery or, rather, a miracle. After their defeat at Bailén, the French abandoned the first siege of the city in mid-August, 1808, leaving its defenders until December of that year to prepare for new assaults. Volunteers flocked to Zaragoza from all over the Peninsula: Aragonese and Valencian peasants in rope-soled shoes, with bright-colored handkerchiefs bound about their heads, swarthy Murcians, Catalans wearing wide, bright sashes, young dandies from Madrid with their swords and the inevitable great cloaks, a Swiss regiment recruited in Aragon, men of a royal sharp-shooting regiment. Earthworks rose about the city; arms and ammunition were cached in heavy-walled convents and churches; food was stored in deep cellars. The Zaragozans went through the neighboring countryside destroying their olive groves so the enemy could find no shelter there—yet an olive tree takes years to mature and bear, and the land about Zaragoza is not rich in other crops. When the French attacked, twenty thousand strong, the city was ready.

Bit by bit, the French bombardment shattered earthworks and walls. Here, the side of a monastery fell upon its defenders; there, a church was blown up. The defenders threw their dead into breaches in the walls in order to hold on a little longer. When a house was taken, they fought from the next house. When a room in a house was occupied, they retreated to the adjoining room and fought from there, sometimes until all were killed or wounded. They fought from street to street; they fought inside churches, the French sometimes firing from behind the high altar and the Spaniards replying from the confessionals, side chapels and the choir.

Young girls from the convent schools worked in the ammunition factory; their mothers and sisters helped the nuns nurse the wounded; women carried food to defenders of exposed outposts and some women even fought beside the men. Fifty thousand, some say sixty thousand men, women and children died of wounds and epidemic in this second siege. When the French finally overwhelmed the shattered city, they entered between the bodies of unburied dead piled like walls along their route.

The city of Gerona had much the same story, for it withstood a blockade of seven months, surrendering only when starvation and disease helped French cannon and land mines to destroy the population.

The war of 1808-1811 goes by two names: the Spanish call it the War of Independence; the English, the Peninsular War. For England, Spain's traditional enemy, came to the aid of the Spanish people, sending the Duke of Wellington with an army to help drive out the French. At last, Napoleon realized that the combined English-Spanish effort had defeated him, and *Pepe Botellas* fled to France. Ferdinand VII, the Desired, returned to a welcoming people.

So far as we know, Francisco Goya y Lucientes did not fire a shot or join a plot to aid the Spanish cause during the struggle. Yet, today, he best expresses the nation's spirit of resistance and shows her sufferings at that time. Appropriately enough, he was born in a little Aragonese town about thirty miles from heroic Zaragoza and spent his teens working under artists in the latter city. He had been living in Madrid for many years when the war came, but went back to Zaragoza in the interval between its two sieges. Much that he saw and heard there then he must have sketched and jotted down for use in his series of etchings known as *"Desastros de la guerra"* (Disasters of War.) Artists admire these sixty-five etchings for their perfection of design and execution, but you need not be an artist to find them unforgettable for the horror, indignation and sympathy with which Goya shows war in all its gruesome details. In one of the most famous of the series, called "The Garroted Man," a priest who has been strangled to death leans against a wall, still clutching a crucifix. In other *"Desastros,"* men and women face advancing bayonets, or lie dead where an exploding shell has tumbled them.

These pictures are full of fury and resentment; other series of etchings reveal other sides of Goya's nature. The eighty pictures of the *"Caprichos"* (Caprices) run from mild irony to bitter sarcasm as they point out superstitions and vices of society. Demons and witches, foolish old men and vain old hags, silly girls and moronic young men, nuns, priests, army officers and aristocrats are shown in little scenes where fantasy mingles with fact. Goya's own comments go with each scene. One well-known *"Capricho"* shows a woman pulling out the teeth of a man who has been hanged. Below, Goya wrote: "The teeth of a man who has been hanged are very efficacious for sorceries; without this ingredient, nothing succeeds. What a pity people believe such nonsense."

In *"Tauromaquia"* he has done a series of studies of bullfighting, less hair-raising, but pulsing, nevertheless, with excitement and drama. Goya was a bullfight enthusiast. In his old age, he used to claim that he paid his way from Madrid to Rome as a youth by fighting bulls in the plazas of small towns en route to the Spanish coast.

Goya is a great painter as well as an etcher; his canvases open fascinating windows on Spanish life. We know his pictures of the wretched royal family. He has left us glimpses of all kinds of other people—stilt walkers, gossiping women, harvesters, cardplayers in the

park, children climbing apple trees. Many of these were intended as
designs for tapestries woven by the royal tapestry factory. He has
also left portraits of grandees, ladies of the court and aristocratic children so natural that the sitters seem about to scold, command, ask for
a glass of wine or comment on Goya as an artist. These petulant,
charming women and wistful children, the romantic or tipsy young
men, these older men, whose character is in their faces, bring their
generation to life. No Spaniard except Cervantes discloses such vistas
on so wide and well-populated a Spanish world.

10. CRACKED ENAMEL—MORE BOURBONS

WHEN Ferdinand came back to Spain in 1811, hundreds of patriots who had fought to drive out the French and return him to the
throne were exiled, thrown into prison or put to death because many
of them felt they deserved a more liberal government and expected
more freedom and Ferdinand loathed liberals and their ideals. Perhaps he feared the sting of Goya's paintbrush, for he did not molest
the painter although he is reported to have said: "You deserve exile;
you even deserve the rope, but you are a great artist and we will forget everything." In spite of this feeling, the King sat for several more
Goya portraits. However, the truce between the two men was so un-
easy that finally the old artist decided to go to France, where he spent
the rest of his life in voluntary exile.

For their heroism against the French invaders, the Spanish people
deserved better than the two miserable rulers who afflicted them for
the next half century. Under Ferdinand and his daughter, Isabella

II, who succeeded him, their only reward for loyalty to the crown was royal tyranny and a corrupt government. More than one insurrection intended to force concessions from Ferdinand or the inglorious Isabella flared up and was beaten out, having accomplished nothing. There were a series of such revolts as well as two civil wars, called Carlist Wars, brought on by Ferdinand's brother Don Carlos and his heirs in their attempts to take the throne from Isabella and later from her son Alfonso XII.

When at last the Spaniards rose against Isabella and drove her from the country, they were so disgusted with her behavior that they did not even want to accept her son Alfonso as King. Instead, they invited an Italian prince to try on the crown. He did so, wearing it uncomfortably for two years and then gladly taking it off and going home at a time when the nation was torn by the second Carlist War. Upon his departure, a republic was organized, but it seemed doomed to failure and so Alfonso XII was invited back to Spain. He proved to be a surprisingly conscientious ruler but unfortunately died after only ten years of reign, leaving his wife as Regent for their unborn child— who was to become Alfonso XIII.

While Spain was engaged in her struggle with Napoleon during the early years of the nineteenth century, and afterwards during the confusion of Ferdinand VII's misgovernment, Mexico and the countries of South America had taken advantage of the situation to gain their independence. By 1824, Spain had lost all her New World empire except the Philippine Islands, Cuba and Puerto Rico.

However, these territories, particularly Cuba, were dissatisfied under the harsh military rule imposed on them. By 1898, Cubans and Puerto Ricans had revolted more than once and the United States had come to sympathize with their cause. When the United States battleship *Maine* was blown up in the harbor of Havana, Cuba, the North American newspapers insisted that Spaniards had sabotaged the vessel, and popular feeling in the United States boiled against Spain. Considered soberly now, it is thought the explosion may have been due to some accident aboard ship rather than to any act of sabotage.

Whatever the cause of the sinking of the *Maine,* the incident was enough to plunge the United States into war against Spain on the side of the Cuban rebels—a war that did not last a year. Our forces won some naval victories in Philippine and Cuban waters, and fought engagements on Cuban soil. Then Spain acknowledged that she was beaten and the Treaty of Paris, signed in 1898, gave independence to Cuba, at the same time awarding Puerto Rico and the Philippines to the United States.

The Spaniards were shocked and humiliated by their defeat, astounded to discover how ill-equipped and unprepared their military forces, especially their fleet, had been. However, they realized that the country was better off without the drain of colonies, and thoughtful, progressive men agitated· for national reforms which would restore national prestige. The future looked bright when the regency ended and Alfonso XIII became King at the age of sixteen. He was attractive, well meaning and intelligent; his people loved him and he cared about his country. But his training had not prepared him for modern times or taught that a king could no longer rule alone and as he chose. His refusal to give the people a share in government was one reason for his failure to unite Spain in contentment and prosperity. But there were other causes for the general unrest, such as desire for more local independence in the Basque Provinces and Catalonian agitation for a separate government. Meanwhile, the army fastened itself more and more upon the King until it became all-powerful and then Primo de Rivera, one of the nine hundred generals in Spain, assumed the dictatorship, making Alfonso a mere figurehead. An able man, Primo de Rivera improved conditions in many ways, but he, too, refused to understand or accept the people's yearning for democratic processes and so his dictatorship failed and he went into exile.

Soon afterwards, in 1931, Alfonso quietly abdicated, and left the country. The Second Spanish Republic was formed without bloodshed. At first, most people were so pleased about the new republic and the ease with which it had been established that they called it *La Niña bonita* (the Pretty Girl). As the Pretty Girl grew older, however, she became less attractive; she fell into bad company. Radical elements, such as Anarchists, Communists and hot-headed Catalan Nationalists, infiltrated the high-minded Liberals who had formed the first government, and all sorts of petty tyrannies began to afflict the Spaniards. For example, the labor unions forbade a man to drive his own auto, declaring that not a wheel might turn unless the owner hired a union chauffeur. A girl watering her garden was ordered not to do so again, as such work must be done by union gardeners. On Labor Day in cities like Madrid and Barcelona, no street cars, buses or taxis ran and not a single private car dared appear in the streets.

The discontent grew, people took sides and bloody clashes broke out as early as 1934, with churches being burned and political assaults and murders becoming frequent. In that year, mine and smelter workers in the province of Asturias wrecked the old city of Oviedo from which the earliest Spanish resistance had surged out against the Moors eleven hundred years before. Only Oviedo's six-hundred-year-old cathedral withstood their fury, becoming a fortress where troops of the government held out until help came to them.

In July, 1936, troops in Spain's North African Protectorate of Morocco rebelled against the government of the republic. Moorish soldiers under Spanish officers crossed the Strait of Gibraltar to land in southern Spain proclaiming revolution; garrisons in many sections of the country joined with them. The Civil War had begun. General Francisco Franco commanded these Rebels (sometimes called Nationalists). The government forces, or Loyalists, were less united in command than the Franco troops and contained various groups with widely different aims. For instance, devoutly Catholic Basques allied themselves with Anarchists opposed to any religion; Catalans, so impatient of "Castilian rule" and eager for self-government fought side by side with Communists who sought not only to keep Spain tightly bound together but to deliver her, so bound, to Soviet Russia as a satellite country.

England, France and the United States did not interfere in the struggle, but Russia took over more and more authority on the Loyalist side while Nazi Germany and Fascist Italy gave General Franco substantial help. Nevertheless, this most dreadful of Spain's civil wars was not brought on by outsiders; it began, like all the others, as a purely Spanish affair, the result of the Spaniard's unyielding nature and his touchy individualism.

It [the Civil War] came from the scarcity of water and the excess of fire in the Spanish temperament. Where the ardent sun of Spain dries up the land—not particularly rich in water at that—the parched earth splits open. The well-meaning foreigner, set ablaze himself by Spanish passions, says "This earth here on the right" or else "This earth here on the left, is responsible."
But there is but one earth.*

The war ended in 1939 with the surrender of the Loyalists. General Franco became Head of State and Prime Minister in the new government. Since then, Spain has not had a democratic or representative regime; even the *Cortes* (Parliament) merely suggests laws without having the power to introduce or pass them. The Falangists, or Spanish Fascists, comprise the largest, most influential party and there are also many monarchists who hope to see King Alfonso's son or grandson on the throne some day. It is hard to know what the masses of the people think or want, or what they feel, other than relief. They are still exhausted from the Civil War, for almost every family lost at least one member. The slaughter was terrific: Political murders and executions by both sides cost about eight hundred thousand lives, and some four hundred thousand more persons died in the fighting. The face of the land was ravaged in many places; air raids battered many of the principal cities, bridges were ruined, convents, palaces, churches and universities reduced to charred ruins, priceless architectural relics made rubble.

One of the most impressive reminders of the war is the massive Alcázar (fortress) in the city of Toledo, which is to be left in the ruined state to which it was reduced by a seventy-day siege it endured with its two thousand Nationalist defenders and their families. No

---

* *Spain*, by Salvador de Madariaga. Jonathan Cape, Ltd., London 1943, p. 352. By permission.

monument newly raised could be more effective. As you survey the wrecked stronghold and recall its story, you think how two incidents far apart in time but very near in feeling emphasize the unchanging nature of the Spaniard.

The first took place more than six hundred years ago in Tarifa, Spain's dazzling white southernmost town; the second occurred in Toledo in 1937. The Tarifa story concerns Alfonso Pérez de Guzmán, called *Guzmán el bueno* (Guzman the Good). The hero of the 1937 tale is Colonel Juan Moscardó. The former held the fortified city of Tarifa for King Sancho of Castile against Sancho's rebellious son; Colonel Moscardó commanded the Alcázar of Toledo under orders from General Franco. Guzmán had a son, a little boy; Moscardó's son, Luís, was sixteen. The rebellious prince held the Guzmán child outside Tarifa; attacking militiamen in Toledo had seized Luís Moscardó. The prince sent word to Guzmán that if he did not surrender Tarifa, his child would be killed. The militiamen telephoned Colonel Moscardó that unless he agreed within ten minutes to turn over the Alcázar, Luís would be shot. Guzmán stood on the fortifications of Tarifa and threw down his own dagger: "Use this," he cried. Colonel Moscardó asked to speak to his son on the telephone. When he heard the boy's voice, he said: "Commend your soul to God, my son; cry, 'Long live Spain,' and die like a patriot." They stabbed Guzmán's son with his father's dagger and Luís Moscardó was shot.

Spanish courage has not diminished with the passing of years; the Spaniards still believe in words like glory, honor, love of country, but they cannot agree on the best way to translate such words into action.

11. ON THE MESETA

No people in Europe have built more great castles, churches and monasteries than the Spanish; in no other country will you find so many ancient cities. Some, like Valencia and Barcelona have become modern although they still preserve buildings and even whole quarters which recall the past. Other cities stopped growing centuries ago and lie, usually on some hilltop, like beauties dreaming of the past.

The central *Meseta* (high plateau) is especially rich in old towns which fell asleep, just as they were, centuries ago and have not waked since—or are only just beginning to wake. Ávila is such a city. If you want to walk into the heart of the sixteenth century, go to Ávila with its terra-cotta roofs pushing up against the bright sky from three quarters of a mile above sea level, its circling walls with their gates and round towers intact after eight hundred years. Alfonso VI, the Cid's lord, began these fortifications when he took the city from the Moors. Even the Cathedral forms a part of the fortifications, for its semicircular rear is built into the wall to form another tower, and is pierced by window slits from which archers and gunners could fire down upon attackers.

If possible, go to Ávila in September or May, for the summer sears the town (though even then the dark interior of the Cathedral is cool as a well) and the winters are bitter. At Easter, water often freezes in the gutters, and by October, winds bring down the snowy breath of the mountains to narrow streets and little plazas. But Ávila is an enchanted place of a fine day in May or September, when sunshine burnishes the stretches of convent walls and gilds stone coats of arms over the doorways of large, somber houses, some of which are only shells of buildings with walled-up, weed-grown windows and doorways.

Ávila is haunted by many ghosts of famous Spaniards. Prince Juan, the only son of Ferdinand and Isabella, is buried here, as is Torquemada, the Grand Inquisitor. Here are many memories of Ferdinand and Isabella, of Charles V and of Philip II, all of whom spent much time in the city. But above all, Ávila belongs to Saint Teresa; she is still its ruling spirit. A fascinating spirit at that! Every detail we know of Saint Teresa's life illustrates sixteenth-century Spanish thought and behavior, and yet, though so typical of her time and her people, she is very much of an individual—an unforgettable personality.

Born less than twenty-three years after the Conquest of Granada, in a fine, gloomy house in the shadow of the walls of Ávila, she grew up on tales of the Reconquest. At seven she and her eleven-year-old brother ran away from home, hoping somehow to reach North Africa, be captured by the Moors and martyred. The children reasoned that in this way they could go straight to heaven. They got no nearer Paradise via North Africa than the road below the city, for an uncle found them and brought them home.

Growing older, Teresa at first felt no inclination to become a nun, for she was an attractive young girl who liked pretty clothes and good times. But her sixteenth-century religious zeal convinced her she could save her soul only in a convent and so she entered one of the many in Ávila. Saint Teresa was a many-sided person. She had trances in which she saw terrible and beautiful visions of saints and demons, yet, having also much common sense, she was ashamed to have anyone find her in a trance, stiff and unconscious. Although often sick and in great pain, she was always cheerful—even gay. "God deliver me from sullen saints," she used to say.

When she was fifty-seven, she left the convent where she had spent more than thirty years to found one with a stricter rule and a more devout way of life. Then, soon afterwards, she went out to establish others like it and kept going until she had set up some thirty religious communities in all parts of Spain. "I felt a great dislike of journeys," she wrote, "especially long ones." No wonder! She was continually on the go. She wrote of "fleas, ghosts and bad roads." She and her companion nuns rattled along over dreadful roads in a covered wagon with solid wooden wheels and no springs, through summer heat that distilled the aroma of sage, lavender and other shrubs growing in the hot, dry wastelands; through winter cold so biting it numbed the poor ladies. They almost drowned fording swollen streams; their wagon nearly fell over a mountain cliff; inns were so filthy they often preferred to spend the night in the wagon. Drinking water frequently gave out, and the food they brought along spoiled; at times they could buy nothing to eat along the way—not so much as an egg.

In Ávila you may visit one convent where Teresa went to school, another where she took her vows as a nun, a third which she founded and a fourth built on the site of her family home. Her sayings, the miracles she is reported to have worked, her personal charm are still subjects for conversation in the city.

Another town on the Meseta which evokes the past is Segovia, lying like a tawny cloud above the surrounding land, or like a great ship with the Alcázar at its prow and the Roman aqueduct at its stern. The Roman Emperor Trajan built the aqueduct so well that it has been bringing water to Segovia from the mountains ten miles away for the past eighteen hundred years. Alfonso the Wise, a thirteenth century King of Castile, often lived in the towered, turreted Alcázar, spending many hours at work on the *Crónica general,* his famous history of Spain that begins with the creation of the world and carries down to the time of his father, King Ferdinand III. If you like ancient churches, not one of the Segovia's is less than six hundred years old except the Cathedral and that is a newcomer of the sixteenth century.

Burgos is the city of Ruy Diaz, the Cid. He was born here—you are shown the site of the house. He and Ximena were married in the lovely Burgos Cathedral and are buried in one of its chapels. Here on display is the chest he turned over to the two money lenders of the town as security for gold he needed after his banishment by the King, telling them the chest held treasure and gold. It was filled with sand. So far as is known, he never repaid the loan after his conquests and successes.

Spain is a country rich in beautiful churches, of which the Cathedral of Burgos is one of the greatest. Its towers are like stone embroidery against the sky, and the interior is unutterably beautiful in bronzes and golds, fine iron grillwork, statues and masterpieces of carved wood.

The university town of Salamanca is another lovely place. Seen from across the Tormes River, its silhouette is charming with towers and roofs and golden walls encrusting three low hills. Only half of historic Salamanca remains, because Napoleon's troops destroyed the other half, which contained thirteen out of the city's twenty convents and twenty of the twenty-five college buildings. Lovers of architecture still mourn the buildings that were lost. Those which remain are very beautiful and people imagine what a gem the city would be if it were intact. The buildings in Salamanca are made of a stone which, when it came from the quarries, was soft as cheese, so soft that sculptors could easily carve it into delicate and intricate designs resembling tapestry or the *repoussé* work you see on some silver today. The university itself is in this style—all scrolls, medallions, shields—ornamental as a piece of stone jewelry. After exposure to the air, the stone hardened and yellowed softly to its present enduring golden beauty.

The University of Salamanca is the oldest in Spain, one of the oldest in Europe. Famous scholars came to it in the Middle Ages. During the fifteenth and sixteenth centuries, the Inquisition controlled its every thought, and its professors won themselves a sorry fame by scoffing at Columbus' ideas of a round world; they insisted that since the Bible spoke of the world as flat, it was heresy to think of a globe. They might have brought Columbus before the Inquisition for his ideas if he had not had the support and confidence of Prince Juan's tutor.

In its great days, ten thousand students crowded its lecture halls, disputed in the shade of oak, elm, cypress and acacia or strolled through the arcades which sweep around the splendid *Plaza mayor* (Main Square)—one of the handsomest series of arcades in Spain. Today, far fewer students come here, mostly young men and girls from the region, and Salamanca does not even offer summer courses to foreign students as do the universities of Burgos, Madrid, Valladolid and Barcelona.

Some of the finest fighting bulls in Spain are raised around Salamanca, and in the past, the Plaza Mayor was often blocked off for a bullfight in celebration of some great occasion. What a sight, worthy of a Goya drawing, the place must have been then, with gay silk and damask hangings fluttering from the iron balconies of the beautiful buildings around the square and twenty thousand spectators, in fiesta best, cheering the brave bulls and the brave bullfighters.

Toledo's magic is most potent by night. The later you reach the city, the darker the night, the greater the spell. As your car gropes across a bridge, you see lights flicker over the black waters of the Tagus River below you, and prick out patterns from the rocks looming ahead. Your car climbs steeply, with dark rocks like cliffs to one side and, on the other side, house roofs washing from you like waves in a dream. You keep on climbing, climbing. Then suddenly, the car stops in a not too brightly lighted plaza, and you stumble sleepily into the hotel. The next morning, the first glance from your window continues the night's enchantment, for you look across brown roofs clustering about the Cathedral so thick and jumbled you feel sure they hide all kinds of mysteries.

If you have time, explore the narrow, cobbled streets, lose yourself in their network and try to catch a rare glimpse through the doorway of some grim house into a patio incredibly gay with flowers. Perhaps you may chance upon a small, lost plaza before a little church, where women chatter as they fill clay jars with water from a well. Now and then a peasant rides past you on his donkey, the donkey's woven saddlebags loaded with vegetables or firewood, pottery or a bag of meal.

In your wanderings, you may come on one of Toledo's two ancient synagogues. Though both have been Catholic churches for nearly six hundred years, they seem to be haunted by Jewish ghosts. One is called Santa María la Blanca; the other, El Tránsito. El Tránsito "is a great hall without aisles, with windows in pierced plaster and panels of inscriptions in Hebrew letters; the other, Santa María la Blanca, has whitewashed columns . . . horseshoe arches and arabesques upon the walls. We can imagine Samuel Levi [builder of El Tránsito] with his red beard and long gown . . . looking like an astrologer. And we begin to fill the galleries of El Tránsito with Jewesses in their curious and elaborate headdresses and costumes, styles of dress which have not been seen in Spain for four centuries and more, but their traces exist scattered far and wide with the Sephardim (Spanish Jew)." *

Of course you must visit the Cathedral of Toledo, the richest and one of the most interesting in Spain, a treasurehouse of paintings, carvings, handsome tombs, gold and silver church vessels, and gold- and silver-embroidered, jewel-studded vestments (sometimes made from the robes of ancient kings). If you happen to be present for some religious service you will never forget the slow procession of church-men in their handsome vestments winding to the sound of the organ through the shadowy aisles of the enormous building, past chapels hidden behind iron gratings.

Go to El Greco's house, too, with its bare, simple rooms and the hill garden overlooking the lower part of Toledo. As you stand before the house, staring over roof tops to the river, you compare the brown city below with his unforgettable green vision of it, now in the Metropolitan Museum. The Greek may have painted in a weird, unworldly way but he lived in worldly enough fashion in this house, entertaining the famous men of his day. Lope de Vega was often his guest, and they say Cervantes came to see him, too, from the humble inn where he lodged when in Toledo. This inn, the *Posada de la Sangre* (Inn of Blood) was destroyed in the recent Civil War. Until then, it had changed little from the days when Cervantes may have stood on the

* *Spain*, by Sacheverell Sitwell. B. T. Batsford, Ltd., London, 1953, p. 60. By permission.

second-floor gallery which ran around the patio, observing the rough and lusty inn guests in the dust or mud below: muleteers unhitching their animals, a soldier dismounting from his horse, merchants thankful to be safe in town with their goods untouched by highwaymen.

The Inn of Blood is to be restored to look as it used to, but as you may recall, Toledo's other well-known war casualty, the Alcázar, will remain the ruined shell it now is, in memory of the war.

12. MADRID

MADRID is not old, as Spanish cities go. It was an insignificant village until the sixteenth century, when Philip II thought its central location on the Peninsula important and made it his capital. Even then, Philip, with his interest focused on building the Escorial, thirty miles away, did little to improve the city, and his Hapsburg successors do not seem to have spent much time there. It was the Bourbon kings in the eighteenth century, beginning with Philip V, who undertook vast improvements and constructions in the capital; Philip built the great square royal palace you see rising so impressively above the Manzanares River. Even so, until a century ago, most of Madrid was a maze of narrow streets and poor buildings with dingy courtyards— as its shabby old sections still testify. A hundred years ago every journalist in Madrid poked fun at the filth and neglect to be seen almost everywhere in the capital.

Modern Madrid, with well over a million and a half population, is now the largest city in Spain, having more than trebled in size during the past thirty years. It has dash and style, is clean, well kept, up to date, with subways (very crowded), fine hotels, elaborate government buildings, churches, beautiful apartment houses and private homes. One can hardly imagine now how it must have looked in March, 1939, when the government forces, which had been holding out against General Franco's troops since November, 1936, finally gave up. Destruction was everywhere. Bombs had exploded up and down the broad, tree-shaded boulevards—in the Gran Viá where the most fashionable shops are located, in the oval *Puerta del Sol* (Gate of the Sun), once the hub of all downtown traffic. Many a flower-filled plaza was a shambles; the campus of the University of Madrid, now a showplace with its handsome new buildings, stood in ruins after serving as a front line of defense. However, not only has the university been completely rebuilt but the damage everywhere in the city has been repaired.

Ornate new buildings crowd the skyline—some as tall as twenty-five stories and skyscrapers by European standards. New residential sections spread farther and farther across the yellow landscape. Many are low-cost housing projects that have been put up to accommodate the hordes of newcomers from farms and villages now glutting the city. Construction cannot keep pace with the increasing population and many new arrivals crowd into dilapidated, unsanitary quarters in old parts of the city or huddle together in depressing slums on its outskirts.

The Madrid that the average tourist knows seems far from these sad evidences of poverty; it is a lively and entertaining place. The art collection of the Prado Museum compares favorably with the treasures of the Louvre in Paris. The Retiro Park is a lovely spot in which to walk or drive, with its stretches of green lawns, wooded walks, bridle paths, fountains, artificial lakes and garden restaurants where you dine and dance outdoors in good weather. During the siege of Madrid, the city's freezing inhabitants were too proud of their trees in the park and along the avenues to cut them down for firewood—but they are said to have eaten some of the animals in the Retiro Zoo. This however, is only a rumor, and anyway, now again the zoo has a large animal population.

The Royal Palace deserves a visit for it contains priceless tapestries, a grand staircase that impressed even Napoleon, and some splendid state chambers such as the Throne Room, with cascading crystal lights, the Gasparini Room hung in blue silk with enchanting porcelain fruits and flowers on the ceiling and nearly life-size Chinese mandarins (also of porcelain) guarding each corner, and the Tapestry Room, jewel-bright with hangings, many from designs by Goya. In the latter room the guide shows you a hole in the ceiling made by an exploding Civil War shell, and then he may go on to tell how Napoleon's troops destroyed the factory which made the porcelains of the Gasparini Room.

The exhibits of the Royal Armory are like a series of illustrations for a book of Spanish history. There you may see the golden, jewel-set crowns of Visigothic kings, the sword Pelayo brandished at the Battle of Covadonga, the keys to the city of Granada turned over to Ferdinand and Isabella by the last Moorish king, the banners Don Juan of Austria brought home from Lepanto. Beplumed and shining manikins wear helmets, gauntlets and armor, and carry the weapons of Spain's great warriors. Many suits of armor of Charles V are on display—some gold-inlaid and etched in intricate designs; here is a suit of mail belonging to young Baltasar Carlos—do you recall him in the Velásquez portraits—and here, armor worn by Don Juan of Austria. Here are the arms of Juan de Padilla, leader of the Toledo *comuneros,* whom Charles V put to death for his share in the revolt against "foreign" rule.

Even the most loyal Madrileño does not claim a good climate for his city, although he may insist that its dry, high air is bracing. Two thousand feet up on the Meseta, Madrid is the highest capital in Europe. The city knows intense heat and bitter cold, sudden changes of temperature and cruel, searching winds from the Guadarrama Mountains to the north. In summer, the government moves to San Sebastián on the seacoast in the north, and the foreign embassies go there too. Then the *gente distinguida* (fashionable people) are also supposed to leave town and those who have to stay home are said to avoid their familiar haunts, because they do not want it known they are so unfashionable as to be in town in hot weather.

Heat or cold the average Madrileños endure with Spanish indifference to weather. Few private homes or apartments, except the most modern and expensive, have what we in the United States would consider adequate heat in winter. The lakes in the Retiro freeze hard enough for skating—yet a sunny room is thought to be sufficiently heated in the coldest weather. You are supposed to feel quite cozy if there is a charcoal brazier or a small electric stove glowing near your feet on a winter evening.

Another distinction which means little to a Madrileño is that between day and night. Most of them get few hours of sleep at night, although they do nap during the long afternoon siesta time, when stores and offices all close. About half-past four or five in the afternoon the city wakes again and business reopens, to keep up at a lively pace for many more hours.

About six or half-past six in the afternoon is the time to start out for entertainment. You may want to take a carriage and drive about through the cool freshness of the Retiro, where you see smartly dressed people doing the same thing. You may decide to go to the movies or a *zarzuela,* where matinée performances begin at half-past six. After you emerge from the show into the lively streets about nine o'clock, it is still too early for dinner; no one except a foreigner thinks of eating at that hour. Wait until ten, unless you are going to an evening theater, which begins at eleven. Linger over your meal and then, about midnight, stroll through the brilliantly lighted downtown streets. They vibrate with music, laughter, chatter. People jam the sidewalks, some with small children clinging to their hands. Cold-drink vendors peddle refreshments, old women and small boys sell lottery tickets for a few pesetas each, reminding you how rich the *Premio Gordo* (First Prize) will make you; the grand prize for the Christmas lottery is worth twenty million pesetas, or about a half-million dollars. Beggars of all ages and all afflictions implore your alms.

At cafés on the sidewalk or indoors, the *tertulias* (evening gatherings) are in full cry; groups cluster about tables, some family parties and many gatherings of men, talking, gesticulating, arguing. The air indoors is already thick with tobacco smoke and grows thicker and thicker until you do not know whether your head whirls from its pungent fog or because of the late hour. If you can see through the fog, you notice that most women have disappeared and this has become a world of men. At last the *tertulianos* get up from the tables and drift into the streets, which are still gay with groups coming out of night clubs and theaters. It is half-past two or thereabouts when you return to your hotel. If you are staying in an apartment or boardinghouse, you clap your hands loudly and then stand yawning outside your building entrance until the *sereno* (night watchman) answers your clapping and hobbles round the corner with the key which unlocks the front door. As he wishes you good night (though it is morning) you reflect that the streets and cafés are the real living rooms of a large Spanish city and realize that your Spanish acquaintances, who always take you to a restaurant, café or theater but never to their homes, are really entertaining you where they themselves are most entertained.

The next morning after breakfast of coffee diluted with hot milk (or thick chocolate or tea) and crisp bread or crusty rolls, you may feel like nothing more strenuous than a shopping tour. Madrid has been often praised as a shopper's paradise, for the Spanish are fine craftsmen and Madrid shops sell goods which soon drain your purse— gloves and handbags that make you forget Paris, embroidered linens as beautiful as those you buy in France and Italy, charming pottery. Of course, too, there are fans and high combs and lace mantillas, not merely the long ones but tiny round bits of lace as well, the sort a bareheaded Spanish girl carries in her purse to arrange over her hair when she goes to Mass or just slips into church to light a candle and say a prayer.

You must not miss Madrid's famous Rastro, a kind of gigantic rummage sale located back of the Puerta del Sol. *Rastro* means rake, and raked in here and spread over the sidewalks or arranged upon shelves in small wooden booths is something of everything from junk to treasures: copper warming pans, remnants of old silk, saucerless cups and cupless saucers, a delicate Venetian-glass vase, hand-worked samplers,

rather grimy to be sure but exquisitely done. Small shops along the
street handle more carefully sorted wares: in one of them you may find
the very out-of-print book you have been looking for, or a Dresden tea
service or a painting.

After elbowing and being elbowed by the crowds in the Rastro you
will be tired enough to want a seat at some sidewalk café, where you
order coffee, lemonade or an ice and then sit back to watch small comedies and tragedies of everyday life acted out or suggested by the pass-
ers-by, some of whom look like characters in urgent need of a plot.
Soldiers of General Franco's Moorish guard in white burnooses and
white turbans and men of the Civil Guard with their three-cornered,
patent-leather hats belong in the chorus of an opera, as do the portly
Spanish army officers whose bright blue or red sashes make a very wide
circumference around their khaki-colored tunics. Now and then a
young nursemaid goes by in the picturesque costume of her native
region, with several good-looking children in tow. The girls and women
you see, though not always beautiful or even pretty, have charm and
grace and almost always look well dressed. No matter how poor she
is, how cramped and bare the home from which she comes, a Spanish
woman takes such pride in her appearance that she will spend her last
peseta for something nice to wear.

Perhaps a funeral passes as you watch; the elaborate hearse (black
for an adult and white for a child) is drawn by horses bedizened with
plumes—the more horses and the more plumes, the more important
the deceased. Death in Spain seems a kind of morbid festival and a
family makes any sacrifice to arrange as impressive a show as possible.
Spanish cemeteries are crowded thickets of handsome headstones and
statues.

With Madrid as headquarters there are interesting short trips to be
taken in the neighborhood across the yellow, treeless expanse of Castile. Thirty-one miles to the northwest the Escorial rises on the lower
slopes of the snow-topped Guadarramas. About the same distance to
the northeast lies Alcalá de Henares, whose university rivaled Salamanca in their great days. In 1836, the faculty and student body

moved from Alcalá de Henares to the capital and since then have been known as the University of Madrid. The beautiful, worn university buildings stand in the old town in all the dignity of their great past. Entering through the cobble-paved courtyard of one, you may lunch in a room looking as it must have during the centuries when professors and their best students ate together around a vast, raised fireplace. After lunch you visit the house where Cervantes was born. The palace of El Pardo deserves a visit; it is only nine miles from Madrid, situated among stunted oak trees in rolling land which was once a royal hunting park. The town of El Pardo was destroyed during the Civil War but has been attractively rebuilt and now has a mosque where Moorish soldiers of General Franco's bodyguard worship.

As you take these trips across the lean, hard, dusty countryside of Castile, where now and then a castle or a hill town etches the distance like a mirage, you are impressed by the uncluttered grandeur of the region and reflect how closely Castilian character resembles the landscape. The Castilian, too, is gaunt and grave and stubborn—not gracious like his neighbors in the southern provinces or exuberant like his countrymen to the north and east. Like the land, however, visions and high ambitions ennoble his outlook and no people of the Peninsula have built finer castles in Spain than the Castilians.

13. ANDALUSIA

ONLY a few mountain passes lead from Castile south through the Sierra Morena (Dark Mountains), into Andalusia, as though nature were trying to keep the electric, bitter air of the north out of this delightful part of Spain. When you travel from Castile through the rocky gorges and flower-scented hills of the Dark Mountains into Andalusia you find what most people consider "typically Spanish." Then, like so many before you, you want to be a painter, a poet, a dancer to express your feelings for the bewitching region which means so much to you.

Andalusia means dusty roads winding through avenues of eucalyptus trees and cactus thickets; white towns against the brown-gray-green of burned grasses; olive groves silver in the sunlight; orange orchards unbearably sweet in the hot air; bare hills or snow-capped mountains sharp against the brilliant sky.

Andalusia has the towers of old Moorish towns rising from distant hills; donkeys clog its roads with their slow trains, their saddlebags bulging with wood, hay and fruit.

Andalusia is the region of large estates, and pitifully poor people who work on them; of thin children running after you down a village street begging for pennies; of graceful women wearing, on Sundays and fiestas, the black lace mantilla draped over a high comb. It is the land of fairs, festivals, pilgrimages, gypsies and fine fighting bulls.

In Andalusia, a man addresses compliments to any girl he admires on the street without intending insult; well-bred young girls do not leave the house without chaperones, and even an American woman feels less conspicuous if she is not alone.

Each Andalusian city brews its own enchantment: Córdoba has the mosque and Moorish bridges and narrow streets in the old section. Málaga and Cádiz have balmy air and superb seaside locations— Málaga on the Mediterranean, and Cádiz thrusting its streets of white houses, like long bright fingers, into the blue Atlantic.

As to the city of Ronda—you have never seen anything like it, perched high on its swelling cliffs and broken through the center by the wide, terrifying, rust-red gorge of the River Guadalevín. In Ronda, three bridges across the Guadalevín; the Romans built the oldest and lowest; the Moors the second, while the third or New Bridge is only a little more than 150 years old. White houses rising from the steep sides of the chasm which divides the town have a dizzying view down to the river flowing through its depths. The old part of the town is a steep, up-and-down tracery of wretched streets where dirty children crowd about begging for money, while the suspicious stares of dark men and women recall to your mind the fact that Ronda has been a smuggler's haunt for centuries. There are fine houses in some of these ancient, miserable streets, with beautiful gardens at the back which run part-way down the gorge. The Ronda bullring with its wrought-iron balconies and covered wooden seats is probably the most picturesque in Spain. The smiling old woman who guides you through it may tell you how the famous Ronda bullfighter, Pedro Romero, about 150 years ago drew up rules for the sport that are still observed. He lived at the same time as Goya, who is thought to have had a hand in designing the glittering costumes bullfighters still wear.

You know something about Granada and its Alhambra or Red Castle which the Moors built in an indescribably beautiful site, upon a hill high above the Darro River with the snow-peaked Sierra Nevada range rising far to the south across fertile land. Although Charles V destroyed part of the Alhambra to make room for the palace he built on the same spot, most of its massive Moorish walls still stand, many lovely courtyards remain and there are delicately arched and tiled rooms and high balconies with exquisite views. The Generalife on another height in Granada is a summer palace of the Moorish kings, which still has delightful gardens and views.

Ferdinand and Isabella must have set great store by this city they won from the Moors, for they chose to be buried in the Royal Chapel of its Cathedral. Their immediate successors, the Hapsburg kings, prized the Alhambra and, though they were always short of money, provided enough for its upkeep. But the Bourbons neglected it until it became a half ruin and the shelter of smugglers, thieves and shady characters. Napoleon lodged his troops in it—it was a strong fortress —and when they left, the French blew up several of its towers.

By 1829, it was in a sad state. Then the young American, Washington Irving, fell in love with its romantic grandeur, lived in one of its apartments and wrote his series of sketches and stories about it, entitled *Tales of the Alhambra*. The book so charmed American and English tourists it brought them flocking to Granada; it roused the Spaniards to the realization that they must either take care of the Alhambra or see it fall into ruins. Today, they gratefully acknowledge that Irving did more than anyone else to save their treasure for them. Granada has become rich and modern, thanks to its tourist trade; indeed the courtyards of the Alhambra and the gardens of the Generalife are so crowded with sightseers that you have to look off to the mountains or down into deep woods below the Alhambra if you want to capture the romantic feelings such beauty should inspire.

Although Seville is the metropolis of Andalusia and one of the greatest cities in Spain, it still looks like a picture-book town. It lies in the valley of the Guadalquivir on that river's flat bank and, once upon a time, was the port through which all trade with the Indies passed. French, Italian and Portuguese ships used to come up the river to dock here, but now the chief traffic of the city is between Spain and the Canary Islands.

Seville is a city of patios that are inviting outdoor living rooms. Through iron grillwork doors lining the street you see alluring courtyards: perhaps one paved in pink marble with walls tiled deep blue, where oleanders, roses, cape jessamine bloom in heavy jars about a center fountain. Many streets are so narrow that when a street car passes, you want to flatten yourself against the wall of the nearest house to let it by. Indeed, the *Calle Sierpes* (Street of the Serpents), one of the principal thoroughfares, is so narrow that no vehicles are permitted in it. It is in the Calle Sierpes that Sevillanos gather to talk and shop and sip cool drinks or hot coffee by day and at night. Here, you buy a fan, a high comb, a copy of *Don Quixote,* a lottery ticket, flowers, or a bird in a little wooden cage; here you stay up with the night owls till one or two in the morning. In the daytime canvas awnings are stretched on ropes, like sails, down the length of the street to keep out the fierce sun; at night, the canvas is furled and you walk or sit under the clear sky.

Seville still reminds you that it used to be a Moorish city. For example, the Giralda, the tall bell tower of the Cathedral, was formerly the minaret of a Moorish mosque which occupied the site of the church. The palace of the royal family is the city's Moorish Alcázar remodeled. The palace gardens are beautiful with roses and cypress trees, winding paths edged with boxwood, pools and fountains—and a latticed Moorish summerhouse where it is said Charles V used to sit and drink tea.

Although many cities in southern Spain are famous for their celebration of Holy Week, not one has so well-known a fiesta as Seville, a fiesta for which tourists book hotel accommodations a year ahead. From the Tuesday before Easter until Good Friday the streets are filled day and night with processions of religious clubs, some forty groups of men marching beside their *pasos* (platforms holding religious figures, often statues of the Blessed Virgin), proceeding from their parish churches to the center of Seville, through the Calle Sierpes, into and out of the Cathedral and then home again.

The *pasos* are so heavy that sometimes one hundred men walk hidden under one to support it. The marchers accompanying the floats wear splendid costumes that splash color in the sunshine or under the lights. These consist of long gowns, cloaks and high-pointed hoods brought down to form a mask over the face, in marvelous colors and

combinations of colors. The members of one club may wear a deep red
hood coming down to a purple gown; another may have blue velvet
cloaks with hoods of gold cloth; a third, black gowns and green hoods. .
The ancient statues borne on the pasos, especially those of the Virgin,
have devoted followers, but the most popular of all is probably the
Virgin of Hope, called *la Macarena* because she is kept in a small
church in the Macarena quarter of Triana, Seville's gypsy suburb. La
Macarena is the darling of the poor people and of the bullfighters, who
pray to her before going into the ring and thank her for their successes.
Joselito, a famous young gypsy bullfighter, gave her a valuable ring
every year until he was killed in the ring.

Some of the hooded marchers or those who help carry the pasos are
Anarchists, who may have even taken part in the burning of churches
during the Civil War—yet they are devoted to their own special Virgin
and determined she shall wear the finest gold-embroidered robe, the
most valuable crown, of any statue in the procession; they tax themselves to buy her new finery and ornaments and fight anyone who suggests she is less beautiful than a rival statue.

A procession takes nine or ten hours to pass, because it must move
slowly through the press of onlookers and stop from time to time to let
the paso bearers rest or to allow the statue to receive the salute of a
saeta. "*Saeta*" means arrow, a saeta being thought of as an arrow of
song flashing out as a young man on a balcony begins to sing or a
woman leans from a window and pours out love for the Virgin in song.
The music of street bands, the sound of trumpets, the hubbub of the
crowds hush as the slow, passionate saeta (in part made up as the
singer goes along) pierces the air.

August fifteenth, the Feast of the Assumption of the Blessed Virgin,
is another day of procession in Seville, of house fronts hung with silks
and decorated with flowers, of crowds swarming and deafening bells
clanging from the Giralda. On this morning the Virgin of the Kings is
carried from the Cathedral through the streets. She is the city's patron
saint and deserves to be queen of all Sevillian Virgins because she is
so ancient and has been so brave. The story about her is that the

twelfth-century King Ferdinand III, wanting a heavenly ally in his fight against the Moors, commissioned a famous sculptor to make him a statue of the Virgin. The sculptor set to work, but when Ferdinand sent word he must have the statue within three days he felt he could not possibly complete the work and went away in despair, locking his studio behind him. On the third day, Ferdinand went to the studio, had it opened—and found the finished statue.

After that, the Virgin accompanied the King on all his campaigns; he felt sure she helped him take Córdoba and Seville from the Moors. Once she was wounded in battle; the legend insists that in the eight hundred years since then no amount of painting over will hide the scars you may see on her face as she rides by, wearing a red and gold mantle and a crown of rubies and diamonds which the ever-grateful Sevillanos gave her twenty-five or thirty years ago.

The Feria in April is another gala time. This is a stock show lasting three days, when a bullfight marks every afternoon and dancing enlivens every night until dawn. At that time wealthy Andalusian landowners open their great city houses and fill them with guests from Madrid, Paris, Barcelona; then you see handsome carriages drawn by blooded horses or fine mules clattering through the streets; then young men and women ride horseback about the fair grounds or throng the city in picturesque regional costumes.

A *romería* in Spain is a pilgrimage or trip to the country to the shrine of some popular saint. Many Spaniards make them, but the Sevillanos have the talent for turning their romerías into something startlingly colorful and gay. One such lively trip is the Romería del Rocío, which starts from Seville at Whitsuntide in early summer and, crossing the Guadalquivir, moves through Triana and into the country. Dressed in their best, the girls in crinolines and shawls, the men in stiff, flat-crowned Spanish hats and short jackets, the pilgrims travel in high, two-wheeled wagons. As the long convoy rattles through the countryside it is joined by more pilgrims in other wagons, on foot and on horseback. The outing lasts three days and nights; when the wagons camp for the evening, the pilgrims sing and dance far into the night.

Triana is the suburb across the river from Seville where gypsies and sailors live, a noisy, crowded place where you see people who belong in some sixteenth-century pícaro tale. There, donkey traffic slows down automobiles, mule carts rattle along and men carry great loads of wood or hay or tiles on their backs. There, too, you see many, many harness shops and knife-grinding businesses, for these are two trades which gypsies follow.

There are thousands of gypsies in Andalusia and the neighboring province of Murcia. When these people came to the Peninsula about the middle of the fifteenth century, they liked the south for its warmth, its olives and fruit. They also liked the fine horses and cattle raised there, which they traded to their profit and to the loss of the simple country people. They wandered from place to place following fairs and other festivals, the men making shady deals in horses and mules, the women telling fortunes and selling love potions; they were a ragged, filthy crew who often set upon travelers on some lonely road and robbed and murdered them. In those days, Spanish law kept them from any trade or occupation other than sheep shearing, keeping an inn in some wild, deserted spot or the hardest kind of farm labor. The Inquisition ignored them as beyond redemption and they were almost pagan in their beliefs. George Borrow, an Englishman who spoke their language and knew their ways so well that they took him for one of themselves, wrote that they did not even believe in life after death. "We have been wicked and miserable enough in this life, why should we live again?" a Spanish gypsy asked him.

Gradually the laws governing them became milder and many who ceased their wanderings were allowed to do any sort of work they wished. Some gave up their gypsy language and dress, but in general the gypsies of Spain were like those of other countries in clinging to tribal ways of life. The country people in Spain still distrust and even hate them; during the last Civil War nearly half the gypsies who were still wandering about the land are said to have been set upon and killed.

The gypsy has contributed a good deal to Spain's artistic life, especially in Andalusia, which is gay with gypsy music and dancing—many gypsies, too, are bullfighters. In Granada, they have been almost as much a tourist attraction as the Alhambra or the Generalife. Gypsy women walk about the town in full or ruffled skirts, their coarse black hair piled high, heavy gold earrings hanging low. Visitors go to the Albaicín, the old section of town where they live, to see their homes in caves and watch their dancing. The Albaicín, however, has become commercialized and lives entirely on tourist trade; the gypsy girls you see dancing there wear lipstick and nail polish and the cave homes are not only clean but full of modern conveniences as well.

Nevertheless, there do exist primitive gypsy cave communities in Murcia, the province next to Andalusia, where thousands live in dwellings scooped from the soft clay of low hills, amid filth, sand, dust and African heat.

Even though you may not actually go to Andalusia, one modern Andalusian poet brings the province to you in his writings—so near that you feel its heat, smell its flowers, its cooking oil and blood, hear its music. He takes you to the bullring and the deep gorge at Ronda, down which they pitch the bodies of horses gored to death by the bull, introduces you to gypsies, shows you murders and dances, tells you about Andalusia of the Roman, Visigothic and Moorish past. This poet is Federico García Lorca, who, in his rather short life, wrote poems which seemed to burst from the deepest heart of his native province. Lorca revived the old *romance* (ballad) which had once been so popular in Spain and used the form for telling thrilling tales of love, revenge and warlike deeds. Even before his poems were collected into book form, his fellow-students at the Universities of Granada and Madrid took to reciting them as people in the Middle Ages used to repeat the works of their favorite minstrels. He wrote plays, too, which express typical Spanish courage, scorn for material well-being and Spanish love of honor. Writing only of Andalusia, the Andalusian countryside and Andalusian cities (Granada, Córdoba and Seville were his favorites), he nevertheless seems to typify all things Spanish in his works.

Lorca was killed in Granada early in the Civil War. At first, the Nationalists were accused of his murder but it is now thought the crime was not political; that it was committed by someone with a personal grudge against him. His poetry and plays occupy a high place in modern literature with many of his works translated into English. Here is a taste of what he wrote:

La Guitarra

The lament begins
Of the guitar
It's impossible, useless
To get it to stop.
It weeps monotonously
As the rain, drop by drop.
Or as the wind weeps
On the snowpeak's top.
It is impossible
To get it to stop.
It grieves for things
Far out of sight—
Like the hot southern sands
For camellias white.*

This description of a bullfight in Ronda comes from one of Lorca's dramas:

In the greatest bullfight ever
At Ronda's ancient circus seen—
Five jet-black bulls, for their devices
Wearing rosettes of black and green—
The girls turned up with shrilling voices
In painted gigs and jaunting cars,
Displaying their round fans embroidered
With sequins glittering like stars.
The lads of Ronda came in riding
Affected, supercilious mares,
With wide gray hats upon their eyebrows

* Translated by Roy Campbell in *Lorca, An Appreciation*. Bowes & Bowes, Publishers, Ltd., London, p. 71. By permission of Bowes & Bayes, and Yale University Press (*Federico García Lorca*).

Pulled sidewise down with rakish airs.
The tiers (all hats and towering combs)
Where people had begun to pack
Round, like the zodiac revolving,
Were pied with laughter, white and black;
And when the mighty Cayetano
Strode over the straw-colored sands,
Dressed in his apple-colored costume
Broidered with silk and silver bands
From all the fighters in the ring,
He stood so boldly out alone
Before the great black bulls of jet
Which Spain from her own earth had grown—
The afternoon went gypsy-colored,
Bronzing its tan to match his own.
If you had seen with what a grace
He moved his legs and seemed to swim;
What equilibrium was his
With cape and swordcloth deft and trim:
Romero torrying the stars
In heaven could scarcely match with him. . . .

[Here follows a passage describing how Cayetano kills five bulls]

The circus with the afternoon
Vibrated, in the uproar swaying;
And in between the scent of blood
That of the mountaintops went straying.*

* Ibid. p. 72.

14. IN THE NORTH

WHEN we speak of Castile, Madrid is not the only city we recall, for other important towns of that region immediately come to mind, such as Toledo or Segovia, nor does Andalusia suggest Seville alone. On the other hand, Catalonia and Barcelona are mentioned almost interchangeably because the great city acts and speaks for its province and represents it almost completely. Catalonia has no other important city within its limits. To be sure, Tarragona, not far from Barcelona, was once the greatest metropolis in Spain, with a million inhabitants, but that was centuries ago—in Roman times; today Tarragona is a sleepy provincial town.

Barcelona, the richest and most important commercial city in Spain, is the least Spanish and is essentially Catalan. Catalans differ in many ways from other Spaniards. They lack Castilian gravity and the Andalusian's half-Oriental charm, and their city is like them. Amid Barcelona's noise and luxury you shake off the heavy sense of crumbling grandeur which weighs on Castile, and put aside the dreamy indolence of Andalusia, feeling wholly in the present among these energetic, worldly, prosperous, friendly Catalans.

In spite of modern ways and looks, Barcelona boasts a past running back to Phoenician and Carthaginian times. It was founded in the third century B.C. by Hamilcar Barca, a Carthaginian general, on the site of an earlier Phoenician town and called Barcina for his family. Even after Rome defeated Carthage, it remained a great city—though not so important as nearby Tarragona. The *Barrio Gótico* (Gothic Quarter) has changed little since the fifteenth century, while in the

Museum of the City of Barcelona you see Roman and Visigothic relics from excavations in the city and the neighboring countryside. The Cathedral of Barcelona in the Barrio Gótico stands on the site where first the Visigoths built a church and then the Moors put up a mosque. Although the Cathedral possesses fine stained glass and other treasures, it is darker than most dark Spanish churches—so dark you will probably spend more time outside under the orange and magnolia trees of its cloisters. All about the Cathedral are other venerable buildings, while the narrow streets of the quarter wind past quaint shops and widen here and there into charming, ancient plazas.

Contrasting sharply with the dignity of its old houses, Barcelona has a few buildings that are like fantasies in a film by Walt Disney. The best known of these extravagances is the unfinished Church of the Holy Family, which has not been worked upon for some twenty years. You doubt that an architect today would complete it according to the plans of the original architect, Antonio Gaudí, for the building is a monstrosity of huge streamers, ribbonlike bows, trees, flowers and other objects tangled and tumbled together as though molded from soft sponge instead of stone.

Gaudí was only one of many Catalan artists who during the twentieth century broke the familiar, traditional art patterns to express themselves in new and revolutionary ways. Many others have taken part in this revolt, among them three artists who are especially well known in this country: Pablo Picasso, Salvador Dali, and Joan Miró.

After you realize that Dali is a Catalan (and therefore a rebel) you understand a little better why he has put the perfection of his painting technique to such mad use. In his canvases, bizarre figures, skeletons, crazily twisted trees, watches lying about like limp pancakes—all the rubbish of a bad dream—are painted with the care and polish a Dutch master might have used for some realistic scene. A few of his pictures are less puzzling and more easily enjoyed, such as his bright, almost-empty scenes on a beach near Barcelona and the whimsical double portrait of his wife. Nevertheless, recalling his work as a whole, you agree that Dali has surely kept his avowed intention "to paint like a mad-man."

Critics agree that Pablo Picasso is one of the outstanding artists of our generation. He is a very versatile painter and his various styles make him much harder to recognize than Dali. Growing up in Barce-lona, Picasso felt the stir of the great artistic revival which swept that city in the 1890's in protest against tradition and rigid rules of art. Later on, he became one of the founders of the then-radical Cubist movement which became an art fashion during the teens and twenties of this century.

In more conventional paintings, he tends to caricature people, often distorting the human body by drawing it out long and thin or puffing it up to look almost like a balloon. His traveling acrobats and circus performers are elongated blue figures emerging from a hazy, gray-blue background. They belong to his so-called Blue period. In other paint-ings he has used flat bright colors to give life and gayety to bullfighters, dancers, harlequins and pierrots.

Joan Miró, the third Catalan painter, may or may not be great, yet his pictures give an impression of freedom, youth and happiness. His "Bird with the Calm Gaze with its Wings Afire" is a delight in electric blues and tingling reds. His view of the "Village of Montroig" where he was born might almost be an illustration from some medieval manu-script with its cream-colored houses cluttering the skyline and the fields working out lovely pink, green and mulberry patches.

In government as in art, the Catalans have resented centralized con-trols and for centuries have frequently revolted against authority. They particularly despise what they call "Castilian" rule; the prosper-ous, intelligent citizens of Barcelona will tell you they are Catalans and not Spaniards so long as Castile claims to represent all Spain. They speak for most of the other people of Catalonia when they repeat again and again that they wish to be an independent nation within the framework of some sort of Spanish confederation. They insist that until Ferdinand of Aragon submitted them to the tyranny of Castile through his marriage with Isabella, their state had been as vigorous and important as Castile, and though smaller had been richer and more enlightened. They point to conquests made by the Catalan Counts of Barcelona (who were also Kings of Aragon): the Balearic Islands and other islands in the Mediterranean—there was even a Catalan duchy of Athens in Greece during the Middle Ages. They are still furious when they recall that Isabella and the Hapsburg kings barred them from any share in the discovery of the New World and kept them from all profits of colonization and trade with the Indies.

One argument they use to prove their right to separation from Castile is that they have a different language, for Catalan is not a dialect of Spanish but a language derived from Latin and as fully formed as Spanish, French, Portuguese or Provençal, the old speech of southern France which Catalan most closely resembles. During the Middle Ages, their literature rivaled that of other European countries, with beautiful poetry, excellent romances of chivalry and outstanding historical works. One of the best of the Catalan historians was James the Conqueror, the fabulously tall and handsome, brilliant, brave King of Aragon and Count of Barcelona who conquered the Balearics and annexed the province of Valencia to his realm. Until the beginning of the eighteenth century people of Spain's eastern Mediterranean coast, some of the islands in the Mediterranean and parts of southern France spoke Catalan. After Catalonia made the mistake of supporting the Archduke Charles in his claims to Spain against the Bourbon Philip V, Philip, having won the crown, punished the rebellious province by banning its language in schools, law courts and printed matter. Of late years, Catalan Nationalists have tried to revive its use but without great success, especially now that the Franco government has put certain restrictions on it again.

A city so brimming over with life and enthusiasm as Barcelona naturally spends the same energy on indignation when it is discontented. If Barcelona is not gay and the Catalans are not enjoying themselves, they boil over into hate and destruction. Riots and rebellions have punctuated the quiet of almost every century. The latter years of the nineteenth century saw bloody strikes, bombings and murder; similar disturbances marred the early part of the twentieth century. The 1936-1939 Civil War turned Barcelona into a center of fierce resistance against General Franco and his forces, and the city was bombed repeatedly, enduring a four-day blitz at the end of the struggle which made a shambles of some sections; many a white Catalan village in the neighborhood was destroyed in the fighting and more than one fine old church was burned by Anarchists among the Loyalists or destroyed by Nationalist bombs. Communism complicates the independence movement in Catalonia and makes it hard to prophesy what will happen there in the future.

Spain has other problems of local discontent. For instance, there is the Basque question, with the Basque Provinces also claiming independent status although less persistently. In former days, like Catalonia, they enjoyed freedom from certain taxes and from military service, but they lost these privileges during the nineteenth century. They, too, have a language of their own—the most unusual in Europe.

No one is sure about the racial origins of the Basques, or where their language came from. According to some scholars, they may be the remnants of a race which inhabited the Peninsula even before the coming of the Iberians. As to the Basque language, one theory holds it to be a living version of an ancient Iberian tongue. Most authorities agree that it bears a certain resemblance to what is known of Iberian, but insist that this kinship cannot be proved because too few written Iberian records remain—only a few inscriptions. Some years ago, light flickered over the shadowy past when excavations near Valencia unearthed an Iberian vase decorated with the painting of a sea fight beneath which were inscribed two Iberian words. When Basque meanings were applied to the words, they could be translated as "Battle Cry." However, this was a mere glimmer in the dark, as since then Basque has not helped decipher significant inscriptions with any degree of certainty.

The Basques say their language is so old it was spoken in the Garden of Eden. They also tell you that the devil, wishing to speak Basque, spent seven years trying to learn it. At the end of that time he gave up his studies because he knew exactly three words. When you think of the twenty-five different Basque dialects, its difficult grammar and words full of letters which look all jumbled together—imagine such family names as Zumalcarregui, Zuzagoitia, Goicoechea or Azpilkoeta —you sympathize with the devil in his fruitless study.

The Basques are simple, strong, daring people (they have been smugglers for centuries, carrying contraband goods across the mountainous frontier between France and Spain). They are also narrow, stern, devoted Roman Catholics and fiercely independent. They fought for narrow-minded Don Carlos in the nineteenth-century Carlist civil wars, but in the recent Civil War, devout Catholics though they were, they took sides with the anti-Catholic Loyalists because they had greater hope of winning self-government from the Liberals than from General Franco's Conservatives. In 1937, German aviators, supposedly aiding General Franco's army, almost bombed off the map Guernica, the ancient city where Basque representatives had gathered in council under a sacred oak tree for centuries. This raid caused international scandal, but Guernica has since been rebuilt into an attractive town. Though the original oak is just a shaft of trunk now, a second oak, planted a hundred years ago, shades the traditional meeting place.

A Catholic church, the oak of Guernica, and a *fronton* are three symbols of Basque life which denote their piety, the love of freedom and their devotion to the sport called pelota. Pelota somewhat resembles tennis, although it is an even faster game. It usually has four players, two to a side, who wear a long, curved basket attached to the wrist for catching and sending the ball back and forth across the *fronton,* a cement court enclosed on three sides by high cement walls. As you watch the players bending, doubling, twisting, streaking across the court, leaping halfway up the wall to capture an elusive ball, you believe what you hear—that the sport is so strenuous pelota players seldom live to be old. Every Basque village has its fronton, often backed up against a blank wall of its church, and of course the Basque cities see a great deal of the game. In fact, in all the great cities of

Spain—in Mexico City and Havana too—pelota has become a popular professional sport, with excited betting going on over every game.

Galicia in the northwest, like the Basque Provinces and Catalonia, has a regional speech, although it is merely a dialect of Portuguese. The Galician is a direct descendant of the Celts who came into Spain so long ago, and he looks it—he might be Scotch or Irish; he plays the bagpipes, carries a heavy cane like an Irish shillelagh and clumps through the rain and mud of his misty-moisty land in wooden shoes. He cherishes many superstitions and knows wonderful myths and legends about the wooded mountains, waterfalls, hillside fields and wayside shrines. He is naturally a poet and a dreamer.

In the past, writers of Spanish plays used the Galician as a stock comic character, a servant who was an ignorant, stubborn, stupid and yet sly fellow. Such a caricature does not give a true picture of most Galicians, who, although willing to do hard and humble work, to be stevedores, harvest hands, policemen, sailors, yet are imaginative, intelligent and industrious. Many have risen high in politics, in literature and the various professions. Galicians frequently emigrate to other parts of Europe and to America, hoping to earn a better living than they can coax from their small hillside farms. You realize how many men have left home when you see that women working in the fields outnumber the men, or notice how gloomy the evening *paseo* seems in some small Galician town, with numerous groups of women and girls strolling around the plaza and only a few men and boys.

15. SPANISH OF THE SPANISH

AS we have seen, every region in Spain differs from the next, with
the inhabitants of each possessing striking characteristics of their own.
Over the past one hundred years Spanish writing captured this flavor
of individuality and authors produced plays and novels—especially
novels—that are striking for their portrayal of local color and distinct
local types. Nearly every Spanish novel is so dyed in the color of a
particular region that it could not have been written about anywhere
else. As you read this literature, you move in a world all the more
wonderful because it is so realistic; you share the bleak life of the
Maragatos, those mysterious people isolated in northwest Spain who
are thought to be direct descendants of Tarik's Berbers; you sympathize with the romantic whimsies of an Andalusian courtship, thrill to
the adventures of Basque sailors, go home with fishermen to tall, crumbling houses huddled about the port of Santander, are shocked by the
poverty and suffering in drab back streets of Madrid.

Among the many novelists who wrote between the middle of the
nineteenth century and the outbreak of the Civil War in Spain, one,
Vicente Blasco Ibañez, became famous in this country through English
translations of his works, in particular through his novel, *The Four
Horsemen of the Apocalypse,* an exciting tale of World War I. Although Blasco Ibañez became famous because of this work, he wrote
much better novels about his native province of Valencia, portraying
with warmth and sympathy the men and women who farm small irrigated truck gardens and orchards around the city of Valencia. These

tales retain their fresh charm, whereas *The Four Horsemen* now seems dated.

Along with Blasco Ibañez, Americans became fairly familiar about the same time with the names and works of two Spanish dramatists, Jacinto Benavente and Gregorio Martínez Sierra. English versions of several Benavente plays were produced here, especially after he received the Nobel Prize for literature in 1922. Martínez Sierra deserves to be remembered for *Cradle Song,* his tender play about a girl-baby waif abandoned at a convent door, whom the nuns bring up until she is old enough to fall in love and be married amid their tears and tremulous smiles. As an American movie, *Cradle Song* was popular, and amateur theatrical groups still produce it occasionally.

We must not leave the Spanish theater without mentioning Antonio García Gutiérrez, a somewhat earlier, nineteenth-century, dramatist, whose tragedy *El Trovador,* written in 1853, so impressed the composer Verdi that he used the plot as a basis for his opera *Il Trovatore.* Verdi also wrote an opera based on García Gutiérrez' drama, *Simón Bocanegro.*

After the Spanish-American War of 1898 a group of young historians, philosophers, journalists and critics calling themselves the "Generation of '98" began to question the reasons for Spain's defeat and national weakness. Each and all had remedies to propose, and they wrote histories, books of philosophy and essays of many kinds to air their theories over the next few decades. Their thought undoubtedly helped prepare for the Revolution of 1931 and the peacefully established republic of 1931. At first these thinkers were enthusiastic over the new republic and served in various branches of government, but many grew disillusioned as violent elements, such as Anarchists and Communists, took over a share of authority, corrupting the ideals of democracy for which the Generation of '98 had struggled; a number of them withdrew from office before or during the Civil War and would have nothing further to do with the sadly changed government.

In thinking of Spanish music, a comparison with the fragrances of Spain suggests itself. Botanists say that of ten thousand flowers found

in Europe, more than half grow only on the Iberian Peninsula—not
just in gardens lush with subtropical bloom; barren wastes, too, nourish
thousands of small plants that lift aromatic flowers into the clear air.
Sailors say the scent of Spain drifts out to sea far beyond sight of her
coasts—an indefinable yet unforgettable scent. When you think of this
fragrance of Spain, you recall Spanish songs and dancing; they seem to
diffuse a sense of the nearness of Spain like a heady perfume.

Spanish music and dancing are so fused as to be almost inseparable,
since most Spanish popular airs are danced to, and dancers very often
sing as they move. Spain possesses the richest folk music in the world,
partly because, in her respect for tradition, she has cherished it jeal-
ously. At feria and fiesta, picturesque regional costumes still come out
of old chests, quaint musical instruments pipe and twang and wail for
joy or loneliness and many an intense, dramatic dance stirs a smoky
village tavern or thrills a village plaza or a bit of meadow by some
stream. You hear the sounds of guitar and tambourine, bagpipe, oboe,
mandolin, castanets, sometimes only the clicking of fingers, the clapping of hands and the stamping of feet as accompaniment to countless
popular and classic dances, all Spanish. You may hear and watch the
*jota, malagueña, paso doble, fandango, parranda, rueda, sevillana,
petenera, rondeña, bulería, granadina, bolero, seguidilla, charrada,
giraldilla, arresku, zortzico, danza prima, muneira, ferruca* or the
espata in Andalusia, Aragon, the Basque Provinces or some other
region. Some of these are slow and monotonous, others fast and
strongly accented, gay and passionate. Deep melancholy and even a
sense of tragedy characterize some; there are dances of religious worship, of courtship, of comedy. Different localities rarely interpret the
same melodies in the same way. The Aragonese jota is not like the
jota as they dance it in Castile or the jota of Murcia. The fandango is
one thing in Andalusia and another elsewhere.

As you might expect, Andalusia surpasses the rest of Spain in music
and dance. The gypsies deserve some of the credit for this pre-
eminence. While they did not invent many of the Andalusian dances,
their splendid coordination, sense of rhythm and intensity of feeling

make them superb performers; you associate the flamenco songs and dances in particular with them. Perhaps you recall that the word, originally meaning Flemish came to denote something vulgar and common; by extension, the meaning was then applied to gypsies, whose behavior often shocked the Spaniards. Flamenco music sounds like Hungarian gypsy music, being by turns gay, plaintive, weird and full of tense, sudden pauses. Flamenco dancers perform in the middle of a group of spectators, who keep the rhythm with their clapping hands and stamping feet and cry out rhythmic encouragements such as *ole* (which means that's good or well done, once more, that's it, keep it up, etc.). The dancers often move to this accompaniment only, and to the clicking of their own fingers.

The women wear full skirts, perhaps a dress with many flounces of bright cotton or of white embroidered material with ruffles up the skirt and at the neck and arms. Their great earrings dangle, a flower is tucked in over one ear. Andalusian women dance well even when they are plump and elderly; they dance not just with feet and legs but with every part of the body, above all, their hands and arms.

An English writer takes us to the Feria in Seville to see Pastora Imperio, a Flamenco dancer; it is 1948 and Pastora Imperio is sixty years old:

She applauded every other singer and showed no inclination to perform, but at last and without any visible urging, rose to her feet, spoke to the guitarist, and draped her shawl round her, taking care to leave her hands and arms unencumbered. The first chords of the guitar sounded; she seemed to reflect for a moment with closed eyes, the rhythm quickened, she opened her eyes with the alert green fire in them, while she stamped her feet and achieved the subtle, or, alternately, thunderous rhythms that are only to be heard when the Hindu musicians rattle or strike their drums with their fingers or with the palms of their hands. I have never known so strong a proof of the Indian in the Gypsy. She glided forward like the cobra, erect and gliding on its tail, a movement accompanied with an incessant, quick tapping of her feet, her body held quite stiff, clapping or fluttering her palms together while she leaned her head as though listening to an incantation. She glided in this manner, in succession, to the four corners of the stage, and returning to the center, stamped her feet in another rhythm altogether, like the roll of drums, and started the long-held, wavering cry of the Gypsy singer. Pastora Imperio is the most controlled singer of Flamenco music that I have heard. . . .*

It is to this same Pastora Imperio that we owe the popular work by the Spanish composer Manuel de Falla, *El Amor Brujo* (Love, the Sorcerer) inasmuch as she persuaded De Falla to compose a ballet in which she could both sing and dance. The music illustrates an old gypsy tale about a girl with two lovers, one a ghost whom she wants to drive away by witchcraft. Later on, De Falla prepared the score for orchestra and we often hear it in this form, particularly the thrilling *Ritual Fire Dance.*

De Falla's music has the unmistakable fragrance of Spain. An Andalusian, he spent most of his life in his native province, absorbing its melodies. He rarely borrowed a folk tune but, rather, composed his own songs. They are, however, so typical that they sound like old folk music. He did use some ancient popular airs in his delightful ballet, *The Three-Cornered Hat,* which he wrote from the lively tale of how some Andalusian peasants outwit a too-flirtatious village judge.

Two other modern musicians who have magically recalled the spirit of Spain were Isaac Manuel Francisco Albéniz and Enrique Granados. Although both were Catalans, much of what they wrote is Andalusian in feeling. We know Albéniz best for *Iberia* his collection of twelve short tone poems vibrant with Andalusian rhythms. "Triana," the number in the collection which is often heard, is a lively piece containing a *paso doble,* or two-step. "El Albaicín," the most beautiful of the twelve, is named for the gypsy quarter of Granada, its melancholy strains recalling gypsy music heard on summer nights.

Granados wrote some Andalusia-inspired dances, but he was not so interested in folk music as Albéniz and De Falla and is best remembered for his opera, *Goyescas,* which has a plot suggested by some Goya designs for tapestries. When the Metropolitan Opera presented the world première of *Goyescas* in New York in January, 1916, the

* *Spain,* by Sacheverell Sitwell. B. T. Batsford, Ltd., London, 1953, pp. 18-19. By permission.

composer braved the sea dangers of World War I to attend the opening performance. On the return voyage, his steamer was torpedoed and he was lost at sea. *Goyescas* has also been made into a piano suite rich with brightly colored jewels of sound.

Any consideration of Spanish art should include bullfighting which is not only a sport but an art, ancient and traditional, reflecting Spanish taste and ability and demanding the Spaniard's muscular control and dexterity. Many techniques of a bullfighter resemble a dancer's. His wrists must be strong and supple to give slow grace to passes before the bull with the cape or the *muleta* (a piece of red serge draped over a stick); his footwork should be sure and graceful and his bodily coordination perfect, for the final phase of the fight where bull and matador face each other is a ballet of death. The matador is near death every second of the time he confronts the bull; the more skilful he is, the greater the risks he takes in daring to bring the bull closer to his body.

The bull is doomed even before he charges into the ring through the gate called the Door of Fright. If the matador fails to kill him the animal must be put to death immediately after the fight. This law is made to protect human lives because a bull learns enough in one encounter in the ring to protect himself, and thereafter cannot be lured by the trickery of cape and muleta waving before him to attack the cloth; instead of rushing at the pink and yellow cape or the bright red muleta, he would make for the man and drive his fatally sharp horns through the fighter's heavy gold and silver embroidered costume.

If you can choose the setting for your first bullfight, see it in the two-hundred-year-old bullring at Ronda which is so picturesque a building and where the local society takes bullfighting seriously. The first great professional fighters were trained in Ronda when the sport, or art, was given up by kings and noblemen and became the profession of gypsies and other poor boys. Pedro Romero of Ronda was one of these first great eighteenth-century professionals; his cape maneuvers and footwork form part of the technique which beginners must master before entering the ring.

The Cid was the first bullfighter to be mentioned by Spanish chronicles, although we are told that the Moors brought the practice into Spain with them in the eighth century. Etchings from Goya's *Tauromaquia* show fighters on horseback or afoot in olden days in public squares converted into rings, in double arenas (two fights going on at the same time) or merely in the open fields; he has drawn Moors waving their wide cloaks before the bull in the way a modern fighter manipulates his cape. Great bullfights used to mark royal weddings, births and coronations—Charles V killed a bull in the ring at Valladolid to celebrate the birth of his son, Philip II. These gentlemen fighters were called *toreadores* whereas the professional of today is a *torero*, a general term applying not merely to the matador but to his assistants, the *picadores* and *banderilleros* as well.

The grand fight season opens Easter afternoon (there have been fights by beginners for some weeks before). From then until the middle of November you may see a bullfight every Sunday in such cities as Madrid, Barcelona, Valencia and Seville—with special fights on special occasions—Seville celebrates the Feria with a *corrida* (bullfight) every afternoon. Smaller towns have their fights on religious feasts or other holidays; if the town is too small to have a regular bullring, the main square is barricaded in with heavy carts and trucks to make one.

The corrida, which usually starts at five or half-past in the afternoon, is the one affair in Spain beginning on time; its opening is much too colorful to miss. When the official, called the president of the fight, enters his box, a trumpet sounds and two other officials, wearing cloaks and plumed hats in the style of the sixteenth century, ride across the arena to salute him. Then the three matadors who are to furnish the chief drama of the afternoon appear. They are dressed in stunning costumes: tight breeches laced at the knee and short, tight jacket with enormous epaulettes; they are wearing white, black, yellow, purple or red suits embroidered in gold and silver and much bespangled. Each matador carries his dress cape furled over his left arm during the opening parade (he will not use it in the fighting); these are marvels of fine embroidery—part of Joselito's handsome cape has been incorporated into the red velvet covering of the float for his favorite Virgin of the Macarena in Seville. As the matadors, three abreast, march across towards the president's box, they are followed single file by their respective teams each consisting of two mounted picadors and two banderilleros. All bow to the president, who throws down the key to the bullpen; they return to their side of the ring, the pen is unlocked and the first bull emerges.

The bullfight has been compared to a three-act drama, with the first act belonging to the picadors astride their jaded old nags. As the other toreros retire, the picadors goad the bull with long lances, provoking him to charge again and again. When he has gored several horses and perhaps just missed injuring a picador, the president of the fight gives the signal for the act to end. Now the banderilleros take over and harry the angry animal by driving into his neck the *banderillas,* yard-long wooden sticks tipped with sharp steel points. They are supposed to insert four pairs of banderillas in order to infuriate him and also to lower his neck muscle with the cruel darts. Their act lasts five minutes.

Now comes the matador, the killer. He has fifteen minutes in which to dispatch his opponent. If he is an artist he manipulates the cape with studied grace, flirting with death while he brings the bull charging hither and thither. The crowd loves it when the bull lunges so close to the man as to rip the gaudy satin of jacket or trousers. When the matador takes up the red muleta and his sword in preparation for the fatal climax of his act, he must move with steely precision and, as the bull charges at the waving muleta, brushing by with lowered head, he must plunge the sword into the animal's neck. It should enter high between the shoulder blades and the first thrust should kill. Aficionados call the kill The Moment of Truth.

Most Spanish boys want to be bullfighters. You see them practicing cape work everywhere, on each other, on mild cows in a field. People tell how Juan Belmonte, when a boy living in gypsy Triana, used to swim the Guadalquivir at night with two friends, ferrying a cape, a sword and a lantern before them on a log to keep them dry. Reaching the Seville side of the river, they broke into some pen where fighting bulls were kept, woke a fierce bull and then, while the friends held the lighted lantern, Belmonte practiced passes with the cape against the animal. Some boys as young as twelve have been accepted as professional matadors although usually a novice must spend six or seven years in training and is considerably older than that before he is regarded as a finished artist.

These novices are preparing for the hardest sort of life—hard even when you do not consider the actual peril in the bullring. The matador travels constantly from place to place throughout Spain during a season, usually reaching his destination only just in time to go into action. When he kills his first bull in the sunlight he is apt to be soaking wet; then he shivers in the sharp wind while he waits in the shadows for his turn to kill his second bull of the afternoon or to go in, if need be, to dispatch an animal which threatens or has injured one of his colleagues. Usually, three matadors dispose of six bulls during an afternoon's show. If the matador is inexperienced, tired, nervous or sick, and his movements therefore are jerky or his sword aim poor, then the aficionados hoot at him and hurl down empty bottles, straw seat cushions, anything that comes to hand. But if he is an artist, if he gives a good performance, treating his audience to plenty of thrills before driving his sword with grace and precision just where it should go into the bull's neck, then he becomes the idol of the crowd. His great fight will be the subject for talk in many a tertulia in many a cafe for years to come and he will become a part of Spanish legend.

16. SPANIARDS

MUCH has been said and written about how widely Spaniards differ from one part of the country to another in characteristics and customs, for observers like to discover and discuss picturesque and interesting distinctions. Spaniards do indeed differ, but they also share many national traits, and as you travel about Spain you realize how basically alike they are in spite of regional differences.

In the first place, you probably decide that most Spaniards are good-looking; many critics consider them the handsomest people in Europe. They are undoubtedly the best dressed, for they care about appearances and will make great sacrifices to have decent clothes and look neat and attractive. Usually of medium height, they have well-cut features and a clear skin that is creamy rather than dark, and rarely freckles or burns in the intense sun and cutting winds of their homeland. Their eyes are fine and expressive and though sometimes gray or green—this latter color is considered a mark of beauty—are usually brown; the more lustrous they are the more surely they denote a trace of Moorish blood. They are usually dark-haired, although now and then you see brown, red and golden heads among them. The women are better looking than the men, perhaps because war has drained off many of the best physical specimens among the men. A Spanish girl with her lovely eyes and dazzling skin, her animation, poise and grace of movement almost always has charm and distinction. Of course, Spaniards vary somewhat in type and build from region to region. You may remember the big-nosed Basque and the Irish-looking Galician. The Castilian is apt to be lean; Catalans and Valencians are taller, big-boned and heavier, perhaps because they eat more than do the people on the spare, poor land of the central Meseta of Castile.

Spanish food has one unforgettable national similarity. Despite a wealth and variety of provincial specialties, the cooking is alike in one way—the food is all soaked in olive oil. So all-pervasive is the smell of oil sizzling in today's meal or the stench of rancid oil from yesterday's meal that sometimes you find it hard to associate such unpleasant odors with the beautiful vistas of the olive groves working gray-green designs across the landscape. Andalusian *gazpacho,* a peasant dish which has become popular throughout the country, is a sort of salad concocted of tomatoes, peppers, cucumbers, vinegar *and* olive oil. *Paella*—Valencian *paella* is the best in Spain and one of the specialties of the province—is a dish of rice cooked in—olive oil; it is yellowed with saffron, flavored with garlic, pepper and salt pork and filled with pieces of chicken, shellfish, sausages and green peas. The Galicians, who have a reputation for being excellent cooks, serve you tripe cooked in olive oil with tomatoes, garlic and sweet peppers, while the Basques prepare snails much the same way, and one of the delicacies along the whole northern coast is a casserole of baby eels baked in—olive oil.

Even the *churro,* a kind of doughnut which is almost a national institution, is fried in olive oil. If you want to try churros, order a cup of chocolate at the same time, because the way to eat them is dipped in the chocolate. They used to tell how King Alfonso XIII followed this good old Spanish custom to the disgust of his English queen, who burst out one day: "In England not even a day laborer would sop his bread in a cup of chocolate." The King went on dunking. "And to think," he replied, "that here in Spain the King does it."

If you want to eat typical Spanish food you must be prepared to take it in olive oil; however, if you prefer your olives only in the form of the small, delicious ripe ones served everywhere—and no other way —then you must patronize hotels and restaurants catering to tourists where the national shortening is used very little.

Siesta, tertulia and *paseo* are three terms essential in describing Spanish everyday life. The siesta is that great quiet which settles over the busiest Spanish city for three or more hours after lunch, making it as deserted as the smallest hamlet; metropolis and village alike drowse while their inhabitants go home to *dormir la siesta*—take a nap. If you happen to be driving through the country in the heat of early afternoon, you will probably catch a glimpse of at least one peasant or wayfarer asleep under a tree or in the shadow of bush, boulder, wall—any shelter he can find from the fierce heat of the sun.

The *tertulia* gives the Spaniard a chance to express his natural gift for conversation and air his views to his cronies on every kind of subject from bullfighters to poetry to politics. An evening gathering of friends, as you know, the tertulia more often takes place in a café than a private house because of Spanish disinclination to entertain at home. Only the rich and fashionable open their mansions and give parties. The average foreigner is apt to be entertained by Spanish acquaintances in a hotel, restaurant or café unless family ties or some other close relationship open the doors of a home to him.

The *paseo* is the evening promenade in smaller cities and towns, when women and girls walk in groups of twos and threes around the main plaza in one direction and the men and boys stroll in similar groups in the opposite direction. As the young people meet and pass each other again and again, a glance or a half smile will help carry on a courtship without the need of a single spoken word. After the paseo ends for the evening, the small cities are likely to continue their bright, busy night life along a few streets where there are shops and cafés, but the little towns soon grow quiet and dark as well.

The furtive flirtations of the paseo suggest the over-all attitude towards young girls in Spain. Almost everywhere they are still chaperoned and allowed none of the privileges modern American girls enjoy. Recently, during its summer cruise, when the training ship of one of our American government schools put into the harbor of Santander on the northern coast of Spain the cadet officers arranged a dancing party complete with suitable chaperones, to which a number of the daughters of local families were invited. When the guests arrived—at midnight, only two and a half hours late—they were accompanied by their fathers or brothers (who had not been included in the invitation). In spite of the extra men and the lateness of the hour, the party was reported to have been a great success.

If the American training ship had been in some port in the south of Spain, it is probable the dance could not have taken place at all, as parents would not have permitted their daughters to attend an affair, no matter how well chaperoned, given by young men they did not know all about. Well-brought-up girls in Seville and other southern cities still lead an almost cloistered existence and never appear on the streets except when accompanied by an older person. In big cities like Madrid and Barcelona, among young women who have jobs or are studying some profession at one of the universities, old strict conventions are disappearing and there is less formality and more companionship between boys and girls. However, in general, a girl in Spain does not have dates as in this country, does not go off to the movies or a restaurant with a young man alone. Chaperoned, she meets boys at teas, dances and various other parties; chaperoned, she may attend the theater or a movie with a beau, but never without the chaperone.

Nevertheless, indications are that old Spanish ways are changing and stiffness is slowly melting from family life. For example, a generation ago, Spanish parents speaking to their children used the familiar, affectionate pronoun *tu* (thou) but the children were taught to reply with *usted*, the polite and ceremonious form of "you." In these same families today the grandchildren use "tu" not only to their mothers and fathers, but also to the very grandparents who still expect "usted" from their grown-up children.

Never before have Spanish customs and traditions been exposed to so many influences from abroad, for never has the country known so many European and American visitors as at the present time. Tourists fill Spain's beautiful hotels and fine, government-maintained inns; they penetrate by good main roads (and over some wretched side roads too), to remote places where life has changed little in centuries and where, until now, a foreign sightseer was enough of a curiosity to bring out disconcerting troops of village children to dog his every footstep. In addition to the effect of tourist ways and tourist trade, American air and naval bases now maintained on Spanish soil must also have an impact on Spanish life. The construction and upkeep of these bases mean employment for many Spaniards, while the behavior of American personnel stationed there will demonstrate the favorable and unfavorable aspects of our American culture. Add to all of these influences from outside, the unrest among the Spanish people themselves, perhaps partly due to the Civil War. They are deserting farms and small towns to flood the big cities in hopes of steady work and better pay.

City dwellers soon lose their individualistic, picturesque country ways and the change in the Spanish peasant will mean a loss to society, for today he is the true gentleman of Europe. So poor that he often does not own a plow or a mule, he farms by the most primitive methods; his wife and daughters work beside him in the fields and wash the family linen in the nearest running stream with flat stones for a washboard; sometimes he cannot read or write. Nevertheless, his gift for conversation, knowledge of his locality, dignity, courtesy and above all his personal honesty give him great distinction. Often he is a natural artist: in Andalusia, the farmer, the cattleman, the muleteer improvise songs and poems as easily as they speak, and every Andalusian plays the guitar well.

Spain is sometimes called the most truly democratic country in Europe because duke and peasant, statesman, shopkeeper and mechanic there can and do find common subjects for interest and talk—at the bullfight, on a train, at a fair, in a café. Such easy intercourse is possible because no one forgets his own place in society or is the least ashamed of it; the mechanic is as proud to be a mechanic as the duke could be of his titles and neither would change place with the other.

This clannishness, this sense of the importance of the individual, is so ingrained in the Spanish temper that it even shows in the use of family names. Wishing to distinguish himself as much as possible from everyone else, the Spaniard keeps his mother's surname as well as his father's. This arrangement may seem complicated to foreigners at first but it is easily illustrated. For example, Goya's full name,

Francisco Goya y Lucientes, tells you that the painter's father's name
was Goya, his mother's, Lucientes. (The mother's name always comes
last.) Had he chosen to do so, Goya might have gone by his mother's
name, as did that other great artist, Velásquez. The latter was born
Diego Rodriguez de Silva y Velásquez, his father being a Portuguese
nobleman and his mother belonging to the Velásquez family of Seville
where the family lived. The son probably used his mother's surname
because it was better known in Seville. The poet Lorca was Federico
García Lorca, but he, too, preferred for some reason to be known by
his mother's and not his father's name.

Sometimes a person links both parents' names inseparably; the nov-
elest Vicente Blasco Ibañez never wished to be called anything but
Blasco Ibañez.

Let us work out a further combination. It happens that a famous
bullfighter, Ignacio Sánchez Mejías, married the sister of another bullfighter, Jose Gómez y Ortega (whom aficionados knew as Joselito).
Suppose that the bride's Christian name was María; then, before marriage she was María Gómez y Ortega; after marriage, María Gómez
de Sánchez. If she had a son and named him for his father, the boy
would be Ignacio Sánchez Gómez or Ignacio Sánchez y Gómez (the
"y" merely means "and"; it may be left in or omitted at will). Thus
no one could mistake the son for the father.

The use of *don* and *doña* casts another light on Spanish thinking.
In earlier centuries, these titles of address were reserved for royalty
and high nobility, but gradually Spanish courtesy and each individual's desire to be treated ceremoniously brought the usage down to a
popular level so that now you may dignify any self-respecting man by
calling him *don* and any woman by using *doña* with her name. However, never use these terms without the accompaniment of the Christian name; add the family name if you wish but do not omit the given
name. Lorca would be either *señor Lorca* or *don Federico* or *don
Federico Lorca*.

Hidalgo is also a term betraying the Spanish attitude towards life;
its meaning seems to be bursting with pride. A contraction of *hijo de*

algo (son of someone), it implies that the hidalgo is the son of someone important and distinguished, though not necessarily of noble blood. Cervantes dignified his hero, Don Quixote, by making him a hidalgo, although Don Quixote's income and background compelled him to lead a meager country existence. The King of Spain could grant any subject the right to call himself a hidalgo, a privilege eagerly sought and which was often the reward for outstanding courage or enterprise. A modern Spanish philosopher has said we must think of a hidalgo not as the heir to worldly riches but to that property we call virtue.

This state of mind, this self-respect, is reflected in Spanish conduct. Even the most casual tourist in Spain nowadays brings back some story of a shopkeeper, a taxi driver or a hotel servant, say, who went out of his way to be helpful or scrupulously honest. As a rule, even the poor and humble in Spain are courteous and consider it beneath their dignity to take a petty advantage over anybody; nearly every one of the country's thirty million inhabitants possesses a sense of *pundonor*. If one word could be said to hold the essence of Spanish virtue, it is *pundonor*. Translated, it means the individual's jealous concern for the respect due to him, respect he must deserve through upright conduct; it means his honor and integrity, which he must preserve at the cost of life itself if necessary. *Pundonor* is an arrogant word in its demand for consideration from others, a dramatic word that has been the theme of more than one Spanish tragedy on the stage and off. If you understand people who stubbornly live and die by *pundonor*, then you admire Spain and the Spaniards.

THE END

INDEX